BROWSINGS

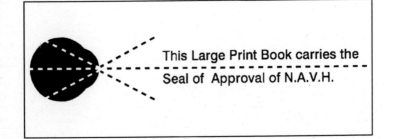

This Large Print Book carries the
Seal of Approval of N.A.V.H.

BROWSINGS

A YEAR OF READING, COLLECTING, AND LIVING WITH BOOKS

MICHAEL DIRDA

THORNDIKE PRESS

A part of Gale, Cengage Learning

GALE
CENGAGE Learning·

Farmington Hills, Mich • San Francisco • New York • Waterville, Maine
Meriden, Conn • Mason, Ohio • Chicago

LIBRARY OF CONGRESS CATALOGING-IN-PUBLICATION DATA

Dirda, Michael.
  [Essays. Selections]
  Browsings : a year of reading, collecting, and living with books / Michael
Dirda. — Large print edition.
    pages cm — (Thorndike Press large print biographies and memoirs)
  Originally published: New York : Pegasus Books, 2015.
  ISBN 978-1-4104-8500-7 (hardcover) — ISBN 1-4104-8500-5 (hardcover)
  1. Books and reading. 2. Dirda, Michael—Books and reading. 3. Large type
books. I. Title.
  Z1003.D5753 2015
  028—dc23   2015029760

Published in 2015 by arrangement with Pegasus Books LLC

Printed in Mexico
1 2 3 4 5 6 7 19 18 17 16 15

*To the memory of Clifton Fadiman,
Randall Jarrell, Cyril Connolly,
and Robert Phelps*

CONTENTS

INTRODUCTION

Between February 2012 and February 2013 I contributed an essay each Friday to the home page of *The American Scholar*. I had no particular restrictions on what I might write about, though it was expected that my column would be literary and personal. Initially I was told that each piece should run about 600 words but, due to my natural garrulousness, this length soon doubled and occasionally tripled. From the start, I planned to write these "Browsings" essays for a year, then stop. And that's what I did.

I've retained the name *Browsings* as the title of this collection, even though it is something of a misnomer. Rather than chronicling "the adventures of a soul among the masterpieces," I quickly gravitated to talking digressively, and I hope amusingly, about bookishness itself. These are, in fact, very much personal pieces, the meandering reflections of a literary sybarite. The essays themselves vary widely in subject matter, and rarely stick closely to their stated titles. In reading them over, I did notice a few repeated names, as well as some dated allusions to contemporary events, but have decided to let these stand. However, I have corrected small mistakes, sharpened sentences and, in one or two instances, added a few illustrative details. But that's all. I hope *Browsings* as a whole will communicate some sense of a year in the life of an especially bookish literary journalist. I also hope that it will encourage readers to seek out some of the many titles I mention or discuss.

Please bear in mind that these are light essays, meant to be entertaining. They aren't jokey precisely, but they do have jokes in them. And lots of allusions and quotations, as well as the occasional pun. Now and again, I go off on rants, sometimes I make up lists, at other times I describe my misadventures at literary conventions and conferences. But throughout you'll recognize, I think, the same voice. If you like that voice, you'll probably like this book.

But allow me to make two small recommendations: First, don't read more than two or three of the pieces at one sitting. Space them out. That way *Browsings* will take longer to get through and you'll enjoy each essay more. Trust me on this. Second, consider reading the columns in the order they appear. Each is meant to stand on its own, but I did aim for a pleasing variety in my choice of topics, as well as a seasonal arc to the series as a whole.

— MICHAEL DIRDA

MR. ZINSSER, I PRESUME

As readers of *Browsings* will discover in the weeks to come, I'm pretty much what used to be called a "bookman." This means, essentially, that I read a lot and enjoy writing about the books and authors that interest me. Sometimes the result is a review, sometimes an essay. But my tone aims to remain easygoing and conversational, just me sharing some of my discoveries and enthusiasms.

Like any sensible person, I'm cowed at the prospect of succeeding William K. Zinsser in this online column for *The American Scholar.* Even as I type these sentences, I'm wondering if there's a way to add a little more dash and color to what I've written. Dickens used to tell his contributors to *Household Words:* "Brighter! Make it brighter!" I can imagine Zinsser saying this to his writing students at Yale, back in the days he taught there.

I read *On Writing Well* when it first came

out, and I've periodically gone back to it since. Having been notably lackluster in my grammatical studies in high school and never having taken any writing courses in college, I have since welcomed all the linguistic counsel and stylistic advice I can get. *On Writing Well* thus stands on a shelf, if only a mental shelf, with such classics as Fowler's *Modern English Usage,* Herbert Read's *English Prose Style,* Robert Graves and Alan Hodge's *The Reader Over Your Shoulder,* Theodore M. Bernstein's *The Careful Writer,* and of course, Strunk and White's *The Elements of Style.*

But *On Writing Well* is more than a guide or even an exemplar of the principles it so attractively preaches. It's also a wonderful anthology of quotations, almost a commonplace book. For instance, the passages Zinsser cites from Alan Moorehead sent me scurrying to locate copies of *The White Nile* and *The Blue Nile,* and then everything else by this superb journalist-historian, now rather forgotten. Happily, any good used bookshop is likely to stock copies of his expertly paced accounts of 19th-century African exploration. Look for the oversized, illustrated editions, which come with maps, period pictures, and much else.

On Writing Well also led me to Zinsser's

own books. Only last year I acquired a copy, in a fine dust jacket, of his first: *Any Old Place With You.* Published in 1957 and winsomely illustrated by Robert Day throughout, it's subtitled "The True Story of Some Impractical Voyages to Implausible Places on a Number of Continents." On the back cover a skinny and very youthful-looking Zinsser sports a white tee-shirt and khakis; his biographical note identifies him as "a man scarcely out of his twenties" and currently a film critic for the *New York Herald Tribune.*

The style of *Any Old Place With You* — the title comes from a song by Lorenz Hart — is breezy and almost relentlessly witty, in the manner I associate with dim childhood memories of riffling through *Holiday* magazine. Here's how it opens:

> One August evening a few years ago, on a park bench in Manhattan, I turned to a willowy blonde named Caroline Fraser, who happened to be turned to me, and spoke the words that started it all: "Let's get married and take a trip to Africa."
>
> Her blue eyes widened, and I searched them for an answer. But I could see only two words: "Drink Budweiser." They were reflected from a blinking neon sign.

It wasn't exactly what I had in mind, but it was something, and I pressed my case. I had been suggesting marriage for weeks, but my proposal lacked that extra detail, like a trip to Africa, that every girl sets her heart on.

"Did you say Africa?" Caroline asked.

"Yes, Africa," I purred, seizing the advantage. "King Solomon's Mines, the Mountains of the Moon, fabulous Zanzibar — it's got everything. Think of Stanley looking for Livingstone, Baker looking for the lost source of the Nile, Clark Gable looking for Ava Gardner."

Before you know it, Caroline has said yes and the new couple is embarked on the Atlantic voyage of the accursed ship *Bahama*. But I should say no more. Find your own copy of the book.

Oh, yes, one more thing, as Lt. Columbo used to say: when I decided to write this opening piece for *Browsings,* I asked my friend Robert Wilson, the esteemed editor of *The American Scholar,* if William Zinsser was still married. "Yes," said Bob. "Her name is Caroline."

[Alas, William Zinsser died at age 92 on May 12, 2015, just as this book was going to press. His death was announced by Caroline Fraser Zinsser, his wife of nearly 60 years.]

STYLE IS THE MAN

In the first of those casual essays that make up *The Spectator,* Joseph Addison declares: "I have observed that a reader seldom peruses a book with pleasure until he knows whether the writer of it be a black or a fair man, of a mild or choleric disposition, married or a bachelor, with other particulars of the like nature that conduce very much to the right understanding of an author."

It's a famous passage, or, at least, it once was. But is *The Spectator* still read today? By that I mean is it read for pleasure, by ordinary people, not just by students in 12th-grade English or by undergraduates taking a course in "Prose of the Augustan Age?" I wonder.

John Steinbeck, you may recall, carried a four-volume set of *The Spectator* on his "travels with Charley." In his autobiography Benjamin Franklin tells us that he taught himself to write by first studying passages of Addison, then attempting to replicate them in his own words. In this he was, of course, following the celebrated advice of the Great Cham himself, Samuel Johnson: "Whoever wishes to attain an *English* style, familiar but not coarse, and elegant but not ostentatious, must *give* his *days and nights* to the volumes of *Addison*."

Back in junior high school, I tried this same exercise with Thoreau, memorizing favorite passages from *Walden* so that I might infuse my eighth-grade book reports with sentences of oaken sturdiness and Shaker simplicity. Decades later, I discovered that E. B. White — the modern master of the plain style — carried a copy of *Walden* in his pocket for many years, like a breviary. As kids say, been there, done that.

Though my heart leaps up when I hear the gorgeous music of 17th-century prose (Thomas Browne, Robert Burton, Jeremy Taylor), such organ-concert grandeur is simply beyond me. If only I had a flair for striking similes and metaphors! Alas, nothing ever reminds me of anything else. Equally elusive are the twists and turns of intricately layered, Ciceronian syntax: I have enough trouble holding a thought in my head for more than a couple of lines, let alone carrying it through serpentine clause after clause. I do sometimes console myself by remembering Isaac Babel's famous dictum: "There is no iron that can pierce the human heart with such stupefying effect as a period placed at just the right moment."

Because of journalism's paramount need for clarity and objectivity, working at *The Washington Post* only reinforced the natural austerity of my prose. An old copy editor I knew used to say, when striking out a needless epithet or intensifier, "No vivid writing, please." Beauty, I learned, grows out of nouns and verbs, and personal style derives from close attention to diction and sentence rhythm. When Yeats decided that his poems had become too ornamented and flowery, he took to sleeping on a board. Before long, he'd put the Celtic Twilight far behind and was producing such shockingly blunt lines as "Nymphs and satyrs copulate in the foam."

In my youthful days as a reviewer, I studiously avoided using the first person singular. With some dexterity, one can achieve a sense of intimacy without it, as *The New Yorker*'s Janet Flanner demonstrated in her wonderful letters from Paris. But the personal essayist needs to master the graceful use of "I." So . . . I try.

A writer's greatest challenge, though, is tone. I like a piece to sound as if it were dashed off in 15 minutes — even when hours might have been spent in contriving just the right degree of airiness and nonchalance. Not that I make it easy on myself to achieve that lightness of touch, given my almost antiquarian penchant for quoting all sorts of authors. See the previous paragraphs for examples.

At all events, let me honor Addison's injunction: I am neither black nor fair but somewhat in between, my disposition tends toward the ironic and self-deprecatory, and I am married with children (now grown). Other "particulars of the like nature" will emerge over time. Onward!

ARMCHAIR ADVENTURES

Why is it that I so seldom want to read what everyone else wants to read? A season's blockbuster will come out — whether Hilary Mantel's *Wolf Hall* or Stephen King's *11/22/63* — and the world will rush off to the bookstores. More often than not, I dawdle instead, take my own sweet time, probably even stop for a coffee on the way. Maybe I'll acquire the new book, maybe I won't.

This isn't to say that the annual prizewinners and best-sellers aren't worth Mr. Bigshot Reader's time or that I think I'm somehow superior to them. On the contrary. I fear that my decreasing interest in the contemporary indicates the onset of old age, or even old fogeyism. Soon I'll start harrumphing when I open the morning paper.

Only partly to my dismay, I find that nowadays I gravitate increasingly to older books and particularly to tales of romance and derring-do from the late 19th and early 20th centuries, the period that the critic Roger Lancelyn Green dubbed "the age of the storytellers."

Last year, for instance, I taught a course at the University of Maryland entitled "The Classic Adventure Novel: 1885–1915," covering 10 books. Given those dates, you can probably guess half the titles on the reading list: H. Rider Haggard, *King Solomon's Mines;* Robert Louis Stevenson, *Kidnapped;* H. G. Wells, *The Time Machine;* Baroness Orczy, *The Scarlet Pimpernel;* E. Nesbit, *The Story of the Amulet;* G. K. Chesterton, *The Man Who Was Thursday;* Rudyard Kipling, *Kim;* A. Conan Doyle, *The Lost World;* Edgar Rice Burroughs, *Tarzan of the Apes;* and John Buchan, *The Thirty-Nine Steps.* If one were to characterize all these disparate works, one might settle for the phrase "comfort books." Other descriptive clichés come to mind: ripping yarns, action-packed swashbucklers, escapist fantasies, boys' books. All accurate designations, but I will make the case that such stories are as important to our imaginations as the more canonical classics.

To my delight, the class proved immensely popular. Students said that it reminded them of why they had majored in English:

not because they could hardly wait to read the latest in literary theory, but because they loved stories. This spring the Maryland English Department invited me back to teach again. Did they want me to take over a graduate seminar devoted to Lydgate's *Fall of Princes*? Lead a class through the complete critical works of Gayatri Spivak? Teach Provençal poetry? Not a bit. Instead of these worthy projects, I'm back discussing "The Modern Adventure Novel: 1917–1973." Our reading list picks up where the previous one left off and includes: Edgar Rice Burroughs, *A Princess of Mars;* Rafael Sabatini, *Captain Blood;* Georgette Heyer, *These Old Shades;* Dashiell Hammett, *Red Harvest;* H. P. Lovecraft, *At the Mountains of Madness;* Eric Ambler, *A Coffin for Dimitrios;* Alfred Bester, *The Stars My Destination;* Chester Himes, *The Real Cool Killers;* Charles Portis, *True Grit;* and William Goldman, *The Princess Bride.*

Despite such plenty, I was chagrined that several titles I really wanted to use were out of print: Cornell Woolrich's *The Bride Wore Black,* for instance, and Lionel Davidson's *The Rose of Tibet.* What are publishers thinking? I could easily have doubled the number of books in both classes. And I still kick myself for forgetting about Kenneth

Fearing's *The Big Clock.*

On the other hand, I frequently find myself remembering the television newscaster and author Heywood Hale Broun. Bear with me a moment. Years ago, Broun would occasionally write for *The Washington Post Book World.* He was, I think, the only reviewer who hand-scribbled his pieces, using yellow sheets untimely ripped from pads of paper intended for schoolchildren. Sometimes his looping script was hard to decipher, but the reviews were invariably dryly witty and quite wonderful.

Broun, I remember from our conversations on the phone, loved old-style "Clubland" heroes, and collected Dornford Yates, E. Phillips Oppenheim, "Sapper," Edgar Wallace, P. C. Wren, A. E. W. Mason, and John Buchan. He reveled in elegant 1920s mysteries set on the Riviera and tales of Graustark and Ruritania, enjoyed old-fashioned thrillers like *The Four Feathers* and *Beau Geste* and *The Pirate Aeroplane* (a favorite of the young Graham Greene), and made no secret that in a better world he would have been Richard Hannay.

Occasionally, Broun would summarize some particularly thrilling plot, and — Lord, forgive me — I would smile, in the superior way of youth, at the old man's boyish enthusiasm. In those days, I much preferred work of the avant-garde to heroic exploits of Napoleon's Old Guard. Had I but known, as the old novelists themselves used to write, what fate had in store for me: Today I'd give a lot to own Broun's adventure library.

Fiction is a house with many stately mansions, but also one in which it is wise, at least sometimes, to swing from the chandeliers. At a dramatic moment in Sabatini's famous piratical masterpiece, the evil buccaneer Levasseur seizes a beautiful captive and snarls: "You do not take her while I live!" To which Captain Blood coolly replies, as his blade flashes in the sunlight: "Then I'll take her when you're dead." Writing — or reading, for that matter — doesn't get any better than that.

Bookish Pets

Poets traditionally own cats. Baudelaire would caress his *"beau chat"* and, being Baudelaire, daydream about his Creole mistress's pliant body. T. S. Eliot famously celebrated the entire species in the comic verse of *Old Possum's Book of Practical Cats*. As a Sherlockian, I'm particularly partial to Eliot's Macavity, his feline Napoleon of Crime, sometimes known as "the hidden paw." Christopher Smart's greatest poem, "Jubilate Agno," memorably extols the virtues of his cat Jeoffry, that "excellent clamberer."

When a young gentleman was said to be going around 18th-century London shooting cats, Samuel Johnson — in Boswell's words — "bethought himself of his own favourite cat, and said, 'But Hodge shan't be shot; no, no, Hodge shall not be shot.' " He wasn't. Later, when the poor creature did lay dying, Johnson gave it valerian to ease its agonies.

My own particular feline companion answers, or rather doesn't answer, to Cinnamon. One of my kids must have given her the name, even though she's mostly peppery gray and white. Originally a stray we took in, the old girl has been a valued member of the household for at least a dozen years. Once, Cinnamon was a mighty huntress, roaming up and down the world at night, seeking whatsoever she might devour — or bring home and lay reverently, as a gift, on the back doorstep. But at some point, the wear and tear of nocturnal outings — of nature red in tooth and claw — became too much for her. I think she suffered a run in with a fox or lost one neighborhood battle too many. At all events, she now stays pretty much inside, sleeping in sunbeams and mewing for food twice a day.

In truth, I'm not really a cat person. Seamus, the wonder dog, still deeply mourned by all who knew him, was just about the only animal I've ever really loved. He died about a year ago now. I always found walking around the block with this happy yellow Labrador among the best parts of the day, a time to clear my head, a time to find new energy and ideas. I miss him. Best dog ever.

Were I more ambitious in the pet department, I would keep tropical fish. Like most people, I find watching the lazy and quiet underwater realm of a big aquarium exceptionally calming. Didn't someone say that he could happily live with the fishes? Was it Whitman? It certainly wasn't Luca Brasi, the Godfather's bodyguard: sleeping with the fishes is quite different. I've just checked, and it was Walt, but not fishes — "I think I could turn and live awhile with the animals . . . they are so placid and self-contained."

I've never been attracted to songbirds. Canaries and parakeets seem so fragile. Dorothy Parker, it's been said, named her canary Onan because he spilled his seed upon the ground. Now and again, I do think a parrot might be interesting, and it would be fun to teach it to squawk a bit of Pirate English: "There's none can save you now, missy." Still, a parrot sounds like more work than a tank of fish. And dirty, too.

The English critic Cyril Connolly kept lemurs — but they were *very* dirty, and in a fecal way. Many years ago, I knew a slatternly blonde who acquired a pet pig, one that followed her around like a dog. It was rather unnerving. Of course, pigs are quite literary creatures: We have Dick King-

31

Smith's Babe and E. B. White's Wilbur and the pigs of *Animal Farm,* some of whom are more equal than others.

Because of Kipling, I've sometimes wondered about keeping a mongoose about the house. But given the cobra population in Silver Spring, Maryland — zero, when last I checked — we hardly need a Rikki-Tikki-Tavi. Still, maybe it would frighten away the deer who eat the flowers and shrubs and the bark from our young trees. As it is, my wife has begun speaking darkly about acquiring a hunting bow. Neither Rudolph nor Bambi would be spared if she has her ruthless way.

Last, but not least, there are horses. Yet somehow these noble quadrupeds don't strike me as pets, despite every young girl's passion for a pony or a palomino. The animals seem too massive, too demanding, and as expensive to maintain as an old Jaguar XKE. William Buckley once summarized what it was like to own a sailboat: stand fully dressed in a cold shower, he said, and tear up hundred dollar bills. Owning a horse appears to be a comparable business. Forgive me, Flicka, Black Beauty, Misty of Chincoteague, and all you other heroic steeds.

Of course, children's literature is a virtual

petting zoo. What kids' book doesn't feature an animal, usually a dog? There's Clifford, Lassie, Lad, Shiloh, Buck, Big Red, Ol' Yeller, and on and on. There are more exotic animals too, such as Henrietta, the 266-pound fowl beloved by Arthur Bobowicz in Daniel Pinkwater's *The Hoboken Chicken Emergency,* or the eponymous protagonist of *My Father's Dragon,* by Ruth Stiles Gannett. Joan Aiken produced a delightful series, exuberantly illustrated by Quentin Blake, about a girl named Arabel and her troublesome raven Mortimer. While Beatrix Potter's little albums are all about animals — especially naughty ones, like Peter Rabbit and Squirrel Nutkin — her woodland characters aren't really pets. They're children in disguise.

In my youth I envied Lord Greystoke (sometimes known as Tarzan of the Apes) for myriad reasons, but partly because of his animal helpers and companions — above all, Jad-bal-ja, the Golden Lion. Still, the most glorious, if unfortunate pet in literature is probably the tortoise in J. K. Huysman's decadent classic, *A Rebours* (Against the Grain). The novel's hero, Des Esseintes, encrusts its carapace with gleaming jewels, then sends this ground-level chandelier lumbering through his mansion's shadowy rooms. Alas, the sad creature, weighed down by diamonds and emeralds, soon sickens and dies.

PAPER

Two weeks ago, in the column called "Armchair Adventures," I happened to mention that Heywood Hale Broun used to scrawl his book reviews on lined yellow paper. What I didn't say, though, was that I recognized that paper. I'd used similar Goldenrod sheets throughout elementary school.

Every September, kids would stop by W. T. Grant's or Woolworth's to buy either Goldenrod or Big Chief school tablets. Today I can't recall if Goldenrod was a brand name or just a color designation, but I do remember a cover artfully decorated with stems of flowers. To the nine-year-old connoisseur, faded yellow paper seemed distinctly classier than Big Chief's dull off-white stock, which was speckled with bits of pulp and little better than newsprint. But whichever style you chose, you did need to hand-punch holes in the side of the pages when adding homework to your three-ring binder. Tough guys would show off by seeing how many sheets they could perforate at once.

Over the years since, I've been slightly obsessed with paper and notebooks. Among my most precious possessions is a small light-blue, breviary-sized volume — four-and-a-half inches wide, seven inches tall — made by a company called Denbigh. There are 140 faintly ruled pages, and about half of them are still blank. This is my commonplace book, into which I copy favorite passages and quotations from my reading. The first entry was made when I was in my early 20s: "How fortunate beyond all others is the man who, in order to adjust himself to fate, is not required to cast away his whole preceding life!" That comes from Goethe, and shows the rather lugubrious worldview of my young Wertherian self.

The most recent addition is an observation taken from the introduction to the *Second Fontana Book of Great Ghost Stories*. Robert Aickman, a master of the genre, is talking about Edith Wharton's most famous supernatural tale: "The important ingredient in 'Afterward' is not the past offense but the truth, reaching far beyond ethics, that we can none of us identify what is crucial until it is too late." I see that my worldview hasn't grown any cheerier since my college days.

Near my desk I keep a large plastic carton filled with fresh notebooks and stationery of various kinds, sizes, and qualities. At one point I owned a few of those ubiquitous Moleskines — the kind supposedly used by travel writer Bruce Chatwin — but they tend to be so expensive that I found myself hesitating to mar their virgin whiteness with my doodles, to-do lists, and earth-shaking, indeed paradigm-altering, observations about this and that. Instead I much prefer school composition books, generally those with austere, speckled black-and-white covers, though in moments of giddy abandon I've sometimes splurged on the versions bound in masculine dark blue or eye-catching neon green. In the fall one can generally pick up such school notebooks at sale prices, often three for two dollars. I usually look for quadrille ruled — the kind with little squares — but these are often hard to find.

Quadrille paper always reminds me of Paris, where I bought similar notebooks from the Librairie Gibert. In them I used to record my various misadventures, set down overheard French expressions and idioms, or add to the list of books recommended to me by the global wanderers I'd meet in youth hostels. In those golden days, I often wore a navy-blue sailor's sweater that buttoned rakishly at the shoulder. Sometimes I'd even sport a dark brown cap called a *casquette.* When sipping pastis and scribbling with my Bic pen, I was sure that I looked every inch an existentialist.

Poking through my box of unused notebooks, many of them scavenged at thrift stores, I see a large red-covered Standard Diary from 2005, a light green-backed record book from the Federal Supply Service, a large journal of 384 "acid-free" pages, a small black notebook with a ribbon band to keep the covers closed, a dozen student examination "blue books" from the University of Central Florida and the University of Maryland, a couple of very small Oxford Memo notebooks (a gift from the writer Paul Di Filippo), four or five scratch pads from various Marriott and Hilton hotels, and a half dozen reporter's notebooks. These last I pick up at *The Washington Post* whenever I go in to see my editors.

The only kind of notebook I actively dislike is the Steno Pad, entirely because of that vertical line down the middle of the page. I presume it has some arcane secretarial use, but to me it's both ugly and confusing.

Over the past couple of years I've occasionally tried to use my computer's stickies and online calendar for notes to myself, but to no avail. My Great Thoughts arrive all too often while I'm reading or out taking a walk or trying to fall asleep. So I like to be able to reach for a notebook, wherever I am. Almost every time I flip one open, especially if it's horizontally ruled, I find myself automatically murmuring one of my favorite mantras: "If they give you lined paper, write crosswise."

THIS IS A COLUMN

Some years back Neil Gaiman and Terry Pratchett joined forces for a comic novel about the apocalypse called *Good Omens.* Almost immediately, fans of this *jeu d'esprit,* in which the newly born Antichrist is mixed up at the hospital with an ordinary baby, clamored for a sequel. Though it seems unlikely that such a book will ever be written, the two authors do have a title — *664: The Neighbor of the Beast.*

Just saying that title over in my mind makes me smile. It's funny, ingenious, and unforgettable. You can hardly ask for more.

Book titles are definitely tricky. I've brought out several essay collections, but I really like only two of the titles I came up with: *Bound to Please* and *Classics for Pleasure.* The first involves triple word-play, one of the meanings being quite naughty; the other recalls a vinyl record label from years gone by. Both, however, underscore my conviction that we don't read for high-minded reasons. We read for aesthetic, emotional, and intellectual excitement.

Sometimes, on long car trips or while awake at 3 A.M., I make up mental lists, and one of my go-to categories is "Favorite Book and Story Titles." Many of them, as it happens, are also among my very favorite novels and stories, period. Now, without question, my all-time No. 1 title is *Persuasion*, Jane Austen's great novel about second chances. Here are a baker's dozen of others, restricting myself to English and American authors:

The Last Good Kiss by James Crumley
"Casting the Runes" by M. R. James
A History of English Prose Rhythm by George Saintsbury
The Well at the World's End by William Morris
"By the Waters of Babylon" by Stephen Vincent Benét
Captain Blood by Rafael Sabatini
An Armful of Warm Girl by W. M. Spackman
You've Had Your Time by Anthony Burgess
Pavane by Keith Roberts
Trent's Last Case by E. C. Bentley

41

The Man Who Was Thursday by G. K.
  Chesterton
Sanctuary by William Faulkner
Naked Once More by Elizabeth Peters
The Door Into Summer by Robert A. Hein-
  lein

Looking over the list, I note that I gravitate
to concise, even one-word titles, so long as
they provide a *frisson* of wistfulness or
bravado or humor. In my younger days I
favored much more poetic phrases like *Tender is the Night* and *Appointment in Samarra,*
but these now seem just a tad melodramatic.
Organizations, pieces of music, and art
works obviously have titles too. For instance,
I don't think you can find a better name for
a newspaper than the Youngstown *Vindica-
tor.* By contrast, all those *Posts* and *Times*
and *Tribunes* seem utterly bland. Consider,
too, the thrilling nicknames for Carl
Nielsen's fourth symphony, *The Inextin-
guishable,* and Mahler's second, *The Resur-
rection.* Two of my most beloved records are
of Elizabeth Schwarzkopf singing Richard
Strauss's *Four Last Songs* and Leontyne
Price performing Samuel Barber's *Knoxville:
Summer of 1915* — haunting titles, even
more haunting music. My favorite painting,
by Watteau, just happens to come with a

wonderful name: *The Embarkation for Cythera.*

Many of the classics in the American Songbook bear tenderly evocative titles: "Anything Goes," "They Can't Take That Away From Me," "Smoke Gets in Your Eyes," "Embraceable You." I think the most romantic of them all, by far, is "The Way You Look Tonight." Then there's that great musical library of love gone wrong — country and western songs — which gives us, among many others, "Ring of Fire," "I'm So Lonesome I Could Cry," and Patsy Cline's immortal ballad, "Faded Love."

But back to books: Perhaps the cleverest of all titles, befitting a Taoist logician who loves paradox and puzzles, are two by Raymond Smullyan: *What Is the Name of This Book?* and *This Book Needs No Title.* Both take their origin, I suspect, from Denis Diderot's 18th-century short story *"Ceci n'est pas un conte,"* that is, "This Is Not a Story" — which only goes to show, as if there were any doubt, that many philosophers are cutups at heart. Still, whatever Diderot's work may or may not be, this really *is* a weekly column, and it's time to stop.

SCRIBBLE, SCRIBBLE

My three sons — all in their early- to mid-20s — can sign their names when they concentrate, but that's just about it. During their elementary school years, Chris, Mike, and Nate were patiently taught the mysteries of cursive handwriting, but since then they've tapped their thumbs on smartphone keyboards far more often than they've gripped a pen or pencil. Though their typing may eventually lead to repetitive stress syndrome, they'll never develop a callus on the top knuckle of the middle finger of their right hand.

My own handwriting is essentially illegible to anyone other than myself, and, after a few days, even I can't always make out the meaning of my scribbles. Deciphering my lists of Important Things to Do would challenge Champollion far more than breaking the secret of the Rosetta Stone. Eminent doctors, envious of a scrawl of such complete and utter opacity, have come to me and humbly asked if I might conduct seminars or offer master classes at medical conventions.

Emily Dickinson told us that success is counted sweetest by those who ne'er succeed, and so it's inevitable that I deeply admire elegant penmanship. Long ago, my friend Sheila Waters — arguably the finest calligrapher in the world — designed the interlocking initials on my wedding announcement; her son Julian Waters, the former calligrapher for the White House, scripted the invitation itself. Their seemingly effortless swirls of ink, their elegant descenders and gorgeous loops, are things of living, interlaced beauty, joys forever.

Inspired by such examples, I've sometimes gone out and bought "calligraphy sets" or pens with italic nibs. I once acquired the simplified booklets of Marie Angel and read through the magisterial *Writing & Illuminating & Lettering* of Edward Johnston. At night I'd practice forming my vowels, carefully mind my Ps and Qs, and daydream about Carolingian minuscule. And, lo!, before long, my handwriting did improve, though no one was ever going to confuse my letters with the timeless italics of papal scribe Ludovico Arrighi.

But handwriting apparently isn't quite like bike riding: it *is* something you can forget if you don't practice. As the upright Dr. Jekyll reverted to the vicious Mr. Hyde, so too my beautiful penmanship gradually degenerated until it once more slouched and shambled hideously across the page. At which point I gave in completely to the dark side. My ink dried up, my nibs clogged, and my Pelikan fountain pen was finally set aside, replaced by disposable ballpoints swiped from Marriott hotels.

Still, I do love what kids facetiously call writing implements. Some travelers collect souvenirs, postcards, or bumper stickers; I bring home a pencil from the various places I visit. In mugs on my desk are pencils inscribed Virginia Aquarium & Marine Science Center, The Morgan Library, Kennedy Space Center, Indiana University, the Space Needle, Villa Emo, Old Capitol Museum (Jackson, Mississippi), The State Library of Ohio, Denison University, and Newport, Rhode Island, among dozens of others. When I pick one up, I remember campuses, certain people, happy times.

Writers, of course, often grow obsessive about their tools. Nabokov composed his later novels on index cards with a Ticonderoga No. 2 pencil. In old age Colette preferred a Parker fountain pen when she wanted to describe the gardens of her childhood with Sido. I myself own an Esterbrook pen that once belonged to Glenway Wescott, author of *The Pilgrim Hawk*. The magus-like Robertson Davies used to sign his novels with what looked like a Montblanc: no author had a more attractive signature. When Terry Pratchett "personalizes" books, usually for hours on end, he asks for a fistful of felt tip pens. Bookstores, being old hands at hosting autograph sessions, usually supply visiting authors with a couple of Sharpies. Dr. Hunter S. Thompson once scribbled in my copy of *Fear and Loathing in Las Vegas* with what might be a thick black marker or crayon: "For Mike, with thanks for getting me the crack cocaine in Boston. Your friend, Hunter."

Still, I guess my own favorite "writing implement" remains a very battered carpenter's pencil. Made by Craftsman and inscribed "America's Highest Quality Tools — Medium," it looks like one of those large wooden pencils used by very young children, but one that has been pressed flat. This is so you can set the pencil down anywhere, even on a pitched roof, and it won't roll away. The wood casing is bright red — for extra-visibility — and the only way to sharpen the blunt graphite is with a knife. I used pencils like this for several summers when I worked for a home improvement company, wore a leather nail apron, and carried a 20-oz. hammer on a loop next to my hip. Today I keep a lone survivor of those hot July days as a memento, but also as a reminder that good carpentry, of any kind, demands a close attention to detail.

Soon after starting at M&M Home Improvement, I grumbled one particularly miserable afternoon — when everything seemed to be going wrong — that a two-by-four I'd just sawn was the wrong length. An old carpenter from West Virginia immediately quipped that I'd "cut it twice already and it was still too short." If you want to work efficiently, he explained, you can't be slapdash. Measure precisely, mark your saw-cuts carefully, then double-check everything. Sound advice, I think, even for those who try to build readable paragraphs rather than fancy additions and back-yard decks.

BOOKS ON BOOKS

I never collected books in a serious way until my mid-20s. On a long-ago trip through upstate New York, my then-girlfriend (now my wife) and I happened to call on an old bookseller named Roger Butterfield. Probably enchanted by Marian, Butterfield invited us to have coffee in his specially built "office" — it was half book barn, half gentleman's study, and completely wonderful. I yearn for something like it to this day.

In the course of the afternoon, this former *Life* magazine journalist suggested a half dozen "books about books" that I should read and, being a docile young man and eager to learn, I went out and read them. These included David Randall's *Dukedom Large Enough,* an elegant memoir of the author's years working in Scribner's rare book department; Charles Everitt's lively and opinionated *Adventures of a Treasure*

Hunter; and Edwin Wolf and John Fleming's sober biography of that dealer in only the rarest of literary rarities, A. S. W. Rosenbach. Later, in Washington, I enjoyed Percy Muir's reprinted radio talks on collecting and John Carter's magisterial lectures, *Taste and Technique in Book Collecting.* One day I even bought my own copy of Carter's *ABC for Book Collectors,* among the most entertaining of all lexicons.

These days I don't read very often about the "gentle madness," as my friend Nicholas Basbanes dubbed collecting in his case-studies of the affliction. But I still keep a large woven basket by my bedside loaded with a dozen or more "books on books," and these I pick up from time to time, usually at the end of a long day. At the moment that basket contains the following:

Indexers and Indexes in Fact & Fiction, edited by Hazel K. Bell

Iris Murdoch, A Writer at War: Letters & Diaries. 1938–46, edited by Peter J. Conradi

The Glory That Was Grub Street: Impressions of Contemporary Authors, by St. John Adcock ("With thirty-two camera studies by E. O. Hoppé")

Ian Hamilton in Conversation with Dan Jacobson

The Folio Book of Literary Puzzles, by John Sutherland

A Book of Booksellers: Conversations with the Antiquarian Book Trade, 1991–2003, by Sheila Markham

In Pursuit of Coleridge, by Kathleen Coburn

The London Library, edited by Miron Grindea

Second Reading: Notable and Neglected Books Revisited, by Jonathan Yardley

What Can Be Saved from the Wreckage? James Branch Cabell in the 21st Century, by Michael Swanwick

Arnold Bennett: The Evening Standard Years, Books & Persons, 1926–1931, edited by Andrew Mylett

The Pleasures of Reading, edited by Antonia Fraser

Seeing Shelley Plain: Memories of New York's Legendary Phoenix Book Shop, by Robert A. Wilson

Howards End is on the Landing: A Year of Reading from Home, by Susan Hill

As you can tell, I have a distinctly Anglophile penchant. But then the English do carry on the best literary correspondences.

Just recall, for instance, the wildly funny epistolary exchanges between Evelyn Waugh and Nancy Mitford, as when the author of *Brideshead Revisited* confesses to the author of *Love in a Cold Climate:* "My little trip to London passed in a sort of mist. Did I ever come to visit you again after my first sober afternoon? . . . On the last evening I dimly remember a dinner party of cosmopolitan ladies where I think I must have been conspicuous. Were you there? I awoke with blood on my hands but found to my intense relief that it was my own. I sometimes think I'm getting too old for this kind of thing." Then there's the hilarious, politically incorrect *Letters of Kingsley Amis:* "I hope the Tatler asked you," scribbles Amis to poet Philip Larkin, "for your views on Ronald Firbank. I told them he summed up all the crappy things about novels that Saul Bellow left unsummed up, though I didn't put it as elegantly as that."

Of course, no serious Anglophile book-lover should be without *The George Lyttelton/Rupert Hart-Davis Letters* — the bookchat to end all bookchat of a former Eton master and a noted London publisher, both of whom are extremely well read, gossipy, and often grumpy about the state of the modern world. I reread the six volumes every few years. Just recently I enjoyed *The Acceptance of Absurdity,* a chapbook containing the charming letters between English novelist Anthony Powell and American bookseller Robert Vanderbilt, mostly concerned with the publication in the United States of Powell's early comic novels *Venusberg* and *Agents and Patients.* Still, just as good as any of these, and with an American slant, is *Memorable Days,* the correspondence between novelist James Salter and literary journalist Robert Phelps. Don't miss the introduction.

These days, *The Paris Review* has repackaged its long-running series of conversations with authors, and even made them available online. I'm glad for this, and yet the original *Writers at Work* volumes, especially the first three, possessed a magic all their own. As a teenager, I virtually memorized my paperback editions, greedy for insider tips about the literary life. Pound, Eliot, Hemingway, Faulkner, Colette, Waugh — they were all there. What has stuck with me the most over the years is their almost universal insistence on the importance of revision, of revising and revising again. Georges Simenon provided one of the most inspirational interviews: he began by saying that Colette had warned him that his early stories were "too literary" and from that moment on he cut out adjectives, adverbs, and any word that was there just to show off. Needless to say, I treasured those underlined and asterisked trade paperbacks, keeping them in a little nook on my bed's headboard, just above my pillow. I probably hoped they would work some subtle Muse-like influence while I slept and one day I would awake a writer. It goes without saying that I was a weird kid.

And some would say I'm a weird adult. Despite the rising popularity of the downloadable e-text, I still care about physical books, gravitate to handsome editions and pretty dust jackets, and enjoy seeing rows of hardcovers on my shelves. Many people simply read fiction for pleasure and nonfiction for information. I often do myself. But I also think of some books as my friends and I like to have them around. They brighten my life.

TEXT MESS

Early in his writing career Walter de la Mare (1873–1956) — poet-laureate of childhood, master of the subtle ghost story, and idiosyncratic anthologist — produced an eerie novel called *The Return.* Its theme is possession: a man falls asleep by a grave and discovers, upon waking, that he has been transformed into the image of a long-dead suicide.

I don't know much more about the plot, and even that summary might be slightly off, since only this week did I decide to read the book. To do so, I first went rooting around in my basement until I'd unearthed the shelf containing a half dozen or so de la Mare titles. Upon closer inspection of these treasures, I discovered that my copy of *The Return* was a shabby ex-library first edition, published in 1910. Nearby I noticed an old Viking Portable anthology titled *Six Novels of the Supernatural* (1944) edited by Edward

Wagenknecht. It included *The Return.*

A digression: Wagenknecht was a huge de la Mare admirer, especially enthusiastic about *Memoirs of a Midget* (1921), which he regarded as the greatest English novel of its time. (I'm not sure I'd disagree with him, even if nobody seems to read the book anymore: those interested can consult the essay on *Memoirs of a Midget* in my book *Classics for Pleasure.*) Born in 1900, Wagenknecht lived until 2004, publishing a book on Willa Cather when he was 94. I've sometimes wondered if he ever changed his mind about de la Mare or *Memoirs of a Midget.* I hope he didn't. End of digression.

As it happened, *Six Novels of the Supernatural* showcased *The Return.* Naturally, I opened the book, scanned the introduction, and, to my dismay, discovered that Wagenknecht had reprinted a "revised" edition of *The Return* published in 1922. My old bookman's heart almost broke.

I wanted to read my beat-up first edition, if only because this was the way the book initially appeared to the public and because this was the text awarded something called the Polignac Prize. The worn cover, the thick paper, the good printing, the slight foxing, the lending library stamps — all gave the scruffy volume a winningly dilapidated, properly romantic character, suitable for a novel about spiritual possession. The clean, neat text in the Viking Portable seemed antiseptic by comparison. It wouldn't be half as much fun to encounter the story in such a format.

Still, that was the version I probably should read, right? But questions remained. Had de la Mare gone back to improve what he regarded as a juvenile effort? Or had he mucked about with the text to its detriment? And should I follow his authorial wishes? I did have a vague memory that his children's novel *The Three Mulla-Mulgars* (also 1910, a good year for de la Mare) had been slightly toned down, almost bowdlerized, when he republished it as *The Three Royal Monkeys* (1927). Could this be a similar case, and might it actually be better to read the un-revised text? Sigh. Perhaps one of my reference books could advise me about these arcane matters.

But E. F. Bleiler, in his *Guide to Supernatural Fiction,* merely noted, without comment, that de la Mare had reworked *The Return* in 1922. I then consulted an essay on de la Mare by John Clute, our greatest living critic of science fiction and fantasy. Double whammy: Clute revealed that de la Mare had tinkered with *The Return* yet again in 1945, apparently still dissatisfied with its text. But were these changes significant? Clute didn't say. Was I going to have to track down — somehow, somewhere — a copy of this 1945 edition?

Hoping to avoid this, I emailed Mark Valentine in England. Valentine edits *Wormwood,* a scholarly journal devoted to "literature of the fantastic, supernatural and decadent"; he also introduced *Strangers and Pilgrims,* a handsome volume of de la Mare's ghost stories published by Tartarus Press. Had he ever compared the three editions? Alas, he had not. Stymied again.

At this point, I thought of L. W. Currey, the leading American dealer in first-edition science fiction, fantasy, and horror. I went to his website, clicked around until I found de la Mare, zeroed in on one of his several copies of *The Return.* And there, in a description of the book, was my answer: "The author revised the text in 1922, toning down the supernaturalism, and this text was the basis of reprints until the recent (1997) Dover reissue which utilized the text of the first edition." Given Dover's reversion to the 1910 edition, it would seem that critical opinion now favors that text. I could read my beat-up copy, after all.

Most sensible people, I'm sure, never

experience such neurotic compulsions and fussy qualms. They pick up a book at the library or bookshop, or maybe they download its text from Project Gutenberg, and, without further ado, they read it. But, alas, I Am Not As Other Men. I like first editions, though I'll sometimes settle for a later printing if it's within a year or two of the book's original publication date. Only these editions possess that distinctive aura of the original, a glamour that subsequent reissues can never recapture. That said, I do gravitate toward well printed, scholarly treatments of certain classic texts, with lots of notes and a good bibliography. If I'm going to spend my life reading books, I want my experiences to be optimal.

Enough of this. With a burden lifted from my soul, I can now settle down and happily read *The Return.* "The churchyard in which Arthur Lawford found himself wandering that mild and golden September afternoon was old, green, and refreshingly still. . . ."

[Note: I did read *The Return* and later wrote about this unsettling novel, and several other "mystical" fictions, in an online essay for *Lapham's Quarterly.*]

TWILIGHT OF AN AUTHOR

While I love most, not to say all, of James Thurber's cartoons, there are a handful that seem especially choice. An example? Picture a courtroom, with a judge, a startled man in the witness box, and a prosecuting attorney who is pointing, triumphantly, at a large kangaroo. The caption: "Perhaps *this* will refresh your memory?" My absolute favorite, though, depicts a guy sitting hopelessly at a typewriter, surrounded by crumpled sheets of paper, while his wife looks down at him and asks, "Has your pen gleaned your teeming brain?"

Her question is based on a famous quotation from Keats: "When I have fears that I may cease to be/Before my pen has glean'd my teeming brain." Certainly, the fears of that doomed tubercular genius, dead at 25, were wholly justified. But I suspect all authors occasionally sit down at their keyboards or open their notebooks and find that Nothing Happens. Every idea seems stale, every sentence hackneyed. At such moments, writers — whether of novels, essays, poems, or book reviews — adopt various coping strategies.

Perhaps a walk around the block or a new environment will clear the head, reopen the floodgates. For some, a move downstairs to the dining-room table or a weekend escape to a friend's condo on the Chesapeake will be enough. Alternately, one can just hunker down for the duration. Flannery O'Connor resolved to be at her worktable every day between 9 and 12, no matter what. If inspiration struck, she was ready. And if it didn't, she still couldn't leave her desk, and so she might as well scribble away at something.

Occasionally, of course, full-fledged Writer's Block sets in. The harder you try, the worse it becomes. Frustration intensifies exponentially before ushering in a long visit from that *Pilgrim's Progress* favorite, The Giant Despair. His voice echoes in your head: everyone knows you're not any good. Never were, really. Just an untalented phony from the get-go. Face it, you've been kidding yourself for years. Your so-called work is completely hopeless, not even a joke. Whatever gave you the idea that you could write in the first place? Look at this pitiful stuff. No one cares, anyway.

. Sometimes Writer's Block can be overcome with luck, persistence, and various subterfuges. Robert Sheckley, a master of the black-humored science fiction story, suddenly found that his hitherto steady flow of ideas had dried up. There'd been too many drugs, too much hard living. But eventually he started to produce saleable material again by telling himself: I can no longer write real Sheckley stories — that's obvious even to me — but I can certainly turn out *imitation* Sheckley stories. And so he did. For readers these "imitations" were okay, not great, but still enjoyable, still Sheckleyesque.

In effect, this is what many writers gradually end up doing in their later years. More and more, they become pale imitations of themselves, reworking old themes, retelling the old stories, relying on professional smoothness to cover up the lack of freshness and originality. While kindly friends assure them that they've still got it, editors seem to blue-pencil their submissions more and more, or refuse their work altogether because they're "overbooked." Eventually, the day arrives when Robert Frost's "Provide, Provide" pops into the graying head:

"No memory of having starred/Atones for later disregard/Or keeps the end from being hard."

But what's a writer to do? Should he or she just pack it in? How, then, will the rent get paid and what about the car insurance? So you put a Willy Loman shine on your shoes, a Gene Kelly smile on your face, and you soldier on: "Hey, Sid, I was wondering if you could use an article on. . . ."

At night, though, the writer stews, blaming the hated Literary Establishment which refuses to acknowledge real talent. Younger people — nothing but good looks, probably sleeping with the judges — take home the awards and the big fellowships. There really is no justice. Before long, the tab at the local saloon is running into triple digits. If illness strikes, so much the worse, especially with so much left unaccomplished. All you want is to bring out one more book, the one that will finally redeem all the dashed hopes and dreams. "Not since *The Great Gatsby* has any novel so beautifully captured the American experience. . . . These are the poems Keats would have written had he lived. . . . Flaubert would envy such prose. . . . Such essays change forever the way we think about literature." And on and on. But finally, instead of such praise and plaudits, one hears only the rasping voice of the eternal pub-keeper: "Hurry up, please, it's time."

Let me stress, though, that none of this applies to you or me. Nope, could never happen to you or me. Not in a million years.

Provide, provide.

SPRING BOOK SALES

Springtime in Washington brings cherry blossoms, azaleas, girls in their summer dresses, and the Stone Ridge School of the Sacred Heart Used Book Sale. It opens today, April 20, and runs through the weekend.

When I first came to our nation's capital back in the mid-1970s, there were a half dozen major used-book extravaganzas each year. In fact, a good proportion of my library was founded on buys from the Vassar, Brandeis, Goodwill, State Department, and Stone Ridge sales. In those days dealers and scouts would arrive from up and down the Eastern seaboard, and the especially stalwart would start queuing the night before, hunkering down in sleeping bags with Thermoses of coffee and bags of doughnuts. It was said that Larry McMurtry — then owner of Booked Up, a high-end shop in Georgetown — sometimes hired a college kid to camp out at the front of the line, so that the novelist could stroll in just before the 9 A.M. opening, take the student's place, and be among the first through the doors into the school gymnasium.

Casting decorum aside, people would race toward the laden tables, the traditional wisdom being that the really good books would be snatched up within the first 20 minutes. Sometimes this was true, albeit less so now, with the advent of "continuous restocking." I've sometimes even found more interesting titles on the second day of a three-day sale. One year, for instance, I picked up first editions, albeit ex-library, of Ray Bradbury's *The Martian Chronicles* and Isaac Asimov's *Pebble in the Sky.* Each was a dollar. Another time I bought — admittedly for $50 — a copy of *The Good Soldier,* one of my favorite novels, signed by its author, Ford Madox Ford. Because I'm drawn to a lot of writers that few other people still read, I can often find works by, say, Martin Armstrong or T. F. Powys or Gerald Bullett or Stella Benson, authors quickly passed over by fans desperately seeking to complete their collections of John Grisham or Charlaine Harris. Above all, though, big book sales remain marvelous realms of serendipity, and one never knows what will turn up. I once acquired the many-volumed complete works of William Hazlitt for a buck a book. As Larry McMurtry's character Cadillac Jack reminds us in the novel of that name, "Anything can be anywhere."

Despite some serious competition, Stone Ridge has always been my favorite biblioblowout, so I'm glad it's still going strong. [But see below.] While standing in line there one year, I joked with a group of friends that we should design a denim jacket for book collectors. On its back would be the stenciled words: "Born to Read." For a couple of years the Stone Ridge organizers actually had me conduct "bookman's tours" of the gym's tables. In the quiet of the afternoon I'd walk around with a small group of people, pluck titles from Travel or Biography or Poetry or Children's Literature, and explain why these particular volumes were collectible, underpriced, or simply well worth reading.

Sadly, I'll only get to the Stone Ridge Sale this year on Saturday, because of a talk I'm giving at a conference at — lah-dee-dah — Princeton. Still, it's not as though I really needed to bring home any more books. No, what I most cherish is that inexplicable feeling of buoyant youthfulness that overtakes me as I wander among the tables and shelves, gradually filling up one of those sturdy L. L. Bean canvas boating bags. And maybe a box or two as well. After a couple of hours I'll feel grotty and tired and very happy. At the checkout, I'll spring for a coffee and a pastry from the schoolgirls selling refreshments. And come the evening I'll wonder what ever possessed me to shell out good money for half the books in my trove — though a month later I'll congratulate myself on having been so wise as to secure all these really quite remarkable treasures. Memory of their cost will have long vanished. As book collectors know all too well, we only regret our economies, never our extravagances.

[Alas, in 2014 the Stone Ridge School of the Sacred Heart hosted its last used book sale. *Sic transit gloria mundi.*]

MEMORIES OF MARSEILLE

Back in 1970–71 I lived in Marseille, where I taught English at the Lycée Saint-Exupéry. The year before, I had graduated from Oberlin College and failed to win a Rhodes Scholarship — a long shot, at best, given that I played no sports, earned mediocre grades as a freshman and sophomore, and had participated in absolutely nothing extracurricular. It turned out that zeal for learning and boyish charm weren't quite enough for the Rhodes committee.

Somehow, though, I was later awarded a place on a Fulbright-sponsored teaching program in France. I asked to be assigned to a school located anywhere but Paris. In 1968 I'd spent a thrilling May and summer in France — "bliss was it in that dawn to be alive / but to be young was very heaven" — and had quickly realized that Paris was full of university students, tourists, and Americans. I didn't want to see any of these. My goal was to speak nothing but French and to learn the language well. As it turned out, by the time I left to return home to the United States, a native French speaker needed as much as two or three minutes before realizing I was a foreigner. My Marseille accent was even remarked upon.

As an *"assistant d'anglais,"* I taught courses in pronunciation and conversation, sometimes to just a few students at a time. On my first day I was immediately warned never to hold a class if only one person showed up. The school — a "mixed" lycée — was exceptionally sensitive about any possibility of teacher-pupil hanky-panky. I was 21, some of my students were 17, and several of the young women dressed with a sexiness and sophistication that took my breath away.

So I could readily understand the school's concern. But there was another reason: it was at Lycée Saint-Exupéry in 1968 that Gabrielle Russier — in her early 30s — had taught and fallen in love with one of her 17-year-old male students. Their affair, illegal to begin with, was further complicated by the leftist politics and rivalries of the day. In the end, Russier was sentenced to prison for what was called, I believe, *"le détournement d'un mineur."* From jail she sent love

70

letters to her burly and bearded young man and then, after her release, committed suicide when prohibited from seeing him. After the letters were published, they became a French bestseller, the same year that Erich Segal's preppy *Love Story* was the No. 1 American tearjerker. (Ethnologists may want to reflect on what this indicates about the two cultures.) As it happened, I taught the brother of the boy involved in this tragic romance, and a movie about it appeared in the spring of 1971: *Mourir d'aimer (To Die for Love),* starring Annie Girardot.

During that academic year I lived on the school grounds in a small room above some faculty and staff apartments. The bleak dormitory-like quarters on the second floor were largely empty except for me and my fellow "assistants" Uli, who taught German, and Paolo, who taught Italian. Uli usually sported a beat-up leather coat he'd found in a flea market, loved the work of William Burroughs, and was a passionate fan of Pink Floyd and Deep Purple, in particular the latter's concerto for rock band and orchestra. He soon found a girlfriend and moved in with her.

Fine-boned, bespectacled, and aristocratic, Paolo quickly became my close friend. He had brought his Volkswagen

Beetle from Pavia, and we soon took to driving downtown to the Canebière, the Vieux Port, and the Opera House. At this last, I watched Rudolph Nureyev and Margot Fonteyn dance in *Swan Lake,* attended an early performance of Alban Berg's restored *Lulu,* and sneaked into a solo piano recital given by Arthur Rubinstein. At that performance, in the middle of a Chopin piece, a loud voice from the audience suddenly cried out, *Plus vite* — "faster." Rubinstein neither faltered nor increased his tempo.

As it happened, Marseille's red-light district was also located on the streets around L'Opéra. Hence the smirks Paolo and I would occasionally receive whenever we mentioned spending an evening there. Paolo, in fact, grew quite infatuated with one particular *papillon de la nuit* — butterfly of the night — and would operatically fling a rose to her as we drove by her corner on our way to a concert or movie.

As the year went by, I soon began taking my breakfasts at the same working-class café, enjoying a sugary brioche along with my coffee and my copy of *Le Monde* or *Le Canard enchaîné.* I took to wandering fearlessly (and foolishly) through the Algerian quarter at night, and vastly enjoyed the rowdy cosmopolitan swarms along the

Canebière. I drank *pastis,* learned to play the cardgame *La Belote,* ate couscous and bouillabaisse and some far stranger things. I was told that if you spoke the right words there was a place in Marseille where you could dine on human flesh. Who knows?

In my spare time I read the works of Marcel Pagnol, especially the Marseille plays *Marius, Fanny,* and *César,* and such Provençal novelists as Henri Bosco and Jean Giono. Occasionally I'd take the bus to Aix, some 25 kilometers to the north, and saunter up and down its beautiful tree-canopied main street, lined with bookshops, cafes and patisseries. One Saturday I climbed to the top of the Montagne Sainte-Victoire, so often painted by Cezanne; on another weekend I went canoeing at Cassis and almost drowned in the Mediterranean surf. During that year a beautiful older woman tried to seduce me — and so did a 16-year-old blonde student. When a celebration honoring the 100th anniversary of the Commune grew violent, we all ran from the riot police.

On school holidays I traveled, spending part of one break with Paolo and his family in Pavia. There, late one night, my friend — even drunker than I — nonchalantly drove his car off the street and down a wide flight of concrete steps. A short cut, he said, but the Volkswagen's suspension was never the same afterward. At the city's cathedral I happened upon a film crew at work and so was allowed to glimpse up close the bejeweled cases holding relics of Boethius and St. Augustine. The following day Paolo and I sampled the liqueurs at the local monastery — the supposed original of Stendhal's "Charterhouse of Parma."

Later in Florence, where I had traveled on my own, I happened to notice a guy absorbed in *The Golden Bowl* while we both waited in line to sign into the city's youth hostel. Now a longtime editor for Harvard University Press, Lindsay Waters and I are still friends. Like Byron and Proust, I sipped coffee at Florian's in Venice's San Marco square, and later went touristing with two Australian women I met there; they ordered me to read Patrick White. On a subsequent trip to Barcelona and Madrid — then still ruled by Generalissimo Franco — I finished André Malraux's *L'Espoir,* as a fascist youth corps marched in a nearby park, and during one long weekend in Grenoble — Stendhal's hometown and Jean-Claude Killy's — I learned to ski.

All this was a long time ago, and, though I've been back to France, I've never returned to Marseille. Why meddle with a fairy-tale year? Even now I can scarcely believe that I used to visit a hunch-backed dwarf who cut hair in an old garage. You'd climb down into a hole in the concrete floor and sit on a rackety kitchen stool, while the barber walked around you, clipping away and chattering about the perfidy of women. If he'd told me his name was Rumpelstiltskin, I wouldn't have been at all surprised.

HAIL TO THEE, BLITHE SPIRIT!

Last week I was in Manhattan for the Mystery Writers of America awards banquet and, having an afternoon free, dropped by the New York Public Library. I'd already visited the Argosy Bookshop on 59th Street, where I'd browsed through the fiction in the basement and scarfed up a first edition (1880) of Mrs Oliphant's *A Beleaguered City*. This, as some readers may know, is one of the novels reprinted in an old Viking Portable called *Six Novels of the Supernatural*. That anthology should sound familiar since I mentioned it a few weeks back when I wrote about the various editions of Walter de la Mare's *The Return*. The Argosy copy of *A Beleaguered City* was a bit shabby, which meant it was only $25. I was quite chuffed, as the English say, to acquire a first.

Being in an exceptionally good mood, I decided to walk the 15 or so blocks to the New York Public Library on 42nd Street and Fifth Avenue. Beware of such moments of exaltation! My shoes were new, and I soon developed a terrible blister on the little toe of my right foot. It's still bothering me.

But I digress.

The New York Public Library has been much in the news lately because of plans to reconfigure its flagship location. As I understand it, the intent is to turn the "old-fashioned" library into a "21st-century" media center, replacing much of its book collection with computer stations and all sorts of digital technology. To me, this is a deplorable idea. Where else but a library can you check out a real book and sit quietly and read it? Where but a real library will you have available both older titles deserving rediscovery and expensive scholarly works? Sigh. It's not as though people can't already access the Internet from any McDonald's in the land. Nor, so far as I can tell, do any but the poorest people now seem to be without laptops or smartphones. As for the networking young: I recently heard on the radio that teenagers transmit roughly 60 text messages a day. I don't think we need to encourage greater use of digital technology. Why should our libraries supply what we already have in abundance? They ought to make available material we can't readily afford or find on our own.

But I digress again.

The last time I visited the New York Public Library the main hall had been opened up to display the manuscript of Jack Kerouac's *On the Road.* The Beat legend typed on pages fastened together into a single long scroll and seemingly all 120 feet of it had been unrolled for awed visitors. Surrounding it were Kerouac artifacts, photographs, and other memorabilia. It was a terrific show.

This year the NYPL, in conjunction with Oxford's Bodleian Library, had mounted a much smaller exhibition called "Shelley's Ghost: The Afterlife of a Poet." In a darkened room the visitor could peer through glass at Percy Bysshe Shelley's handwritten text of "Adonais," his elegy for John Keats, or study four pages from the manuscript of his wife Mary Shelley's novel *Frankenstein.* There were documents written by Mary's parents, too, the philosopher-novelist William Godwin and the great feminist thinker Mary Wollstonecraft, author of the groundbreaking *A Vindication of the Rights of Woman.* The exhibition even included a waterlogged copy of Sophocles's *Tragedies* — supposedly the volume in Shelley's pocket when his boat foundered in a storm and he drowned at age 29.

However, for me the greatest thrill was seeing a fair copy of "Ozymandias." This is, of course, one of the world's most famous poems, but it holds a special place in my heart. When I was around 13 I happened to acquire, from an industrial dumpster behind a department store, a stack of records that had been discarded (or hidden there by a larcenous employee). One of those vinyl LPs was entitled "Vincent Price Reads the Poems of Shelley."

That afternoon, when I was sure that my parents and sisters were away, I played the record and was electrified. This cognac-smooth, patrician voice echoed through my bedroom: "I met a traveler from an antique land / Who said: 'Two vast and trunkless legs of stone / Stand in the desert. . . .'" The poem, as you will recall, builds to that magnificently defiant proclamation: "Look on my Works, ye Mighty, and despair!" There follows, immediately, the deliciously cynical climax: "Nothing beside remains. Round the decay / Of that colossal Wreck, boundless and bare / The lone and level sands stretch far away."

Well, I was bowled over. If this was poetry, let me have more of it. I played the record again and again, practiced reciting the poems in Price's voice, and memorized three or four of them, including the wonderfully hokey "The Indian Serenade," now better known as "The Indian Girl's Song," which then struck me as the very acme of Romantic love poetry:

I arise from dreams of thee
In the first sweet sleep of night —
When the winds are breathing low
And the stars are shining bright.

I arise from dreams of thee —
And a spirit in my feet
Hath led me — Who knows how?
To thy chamber window, Sweet . . .

O lift me from the grass!
I die, I faint, I fail!
Let thy love in kisses rain
On my lips and eyelids pale . . .

What I didn't know then, when I was declaiming to the tiles of my bathroom, was that Shelley's star had sunk fairly low in the poetic firmament. He was thought to be rhetorical, corny, not quite first-rate. Keats, by contrast — he was The Man. Later, in the 1970s, the young Harold Bloom argued fiercely for Shelley's imaginative breadth and originality, but with only partial success. Even now Shelley sometimes seems admired more as a radical thinker and free spirit than as a major English poet.

No matter. To me, he will always be my heady entry-level drug into a lifelong addiction to poetry. These days, I may prefer John Donne or Wallace Stevens, but I still own that Vincent Price LP and sometimes, when my family is out of the house, I still play it. "I die, I faint, I fail!"

SYNONYM TOAST

Some years back, Oxford University Press decided to bring out a new thesaurus. *The Oxford American Writer's Thesaurus* would be alphabetical (rather than thematic, as Roget's original had been), and it would include tables and inserts detailing the graded differences in connotation among groups of synonyms. Thus, on page 427 of the second edition, published in 2008, one finds a little box explaining the nuances distinguishing such similar words as "honor, deference, homage, obeisance" and "reverence."

To further enhance the new thesaurus, the Oxford editors also asked 10 very different writers to contribute mini-essays on words they loved or hated. These pieces — on words ranging from "achingly" to "yump" — were consequently scattered throughout the *OAWT,* little oases of prose among all the wordlists. The lucky contributors included Zadie Smith, David Foster Wallace, Simon Winchester, Francine Prose, David Auburn, David Lehman, Erin McKean, Stephen Merritt, Jean Strouse, and me.

Sometimes when I use the thesaurus — and, like any shill on the radio, I do use this product myself — I sometimes wonder how many David Foster Wallace fans know about his contributions. He comments, for instance, on the following words: "all of," "as," "critique," "dialogue," "effete," "feckless," "fervent," "focus," "hairy," "if" "impossibly," "loan," "mucous," "myriad," "privilege," "pulchritude," "that," "toward, towards," "unique," and "utilize." Here, for instance, is what he says about "pulchritude" (it appears appended to the entry on "Beauty"):

"A paradoxical noun because it means beauty but is itself one of the ugliest words in the language. Same goes for the adjectival form *pulchritudinous.* They're part of a tiny elite cadre of words that possess the very opposite of the qualities they denote. *Diminutive, big, foreign, fancy* (adjective), *colloquialism,* and *monosyllabic* are some others; there are at least a dozen more. Inviting your school-age kids to list as many paradoxical words as they can is a neat way to deepen their relationship to English and

83

help them see that words are both symbols for things and very real things themselves."

What of my own favorites and bugaboos? I thought you'd never ask. The run of words that annoy me — they range from "brave" and "limn" to "Faulknerian" and "feisty" — is fairly extensive. But here's an entry in praise of "stippled"; it appears near the entry for "spotted."

"*Stippled, flecked, dappled, variegated, speckled, spotted, pied, larded, dominoed, polka-dotted, brindled, freckled* — all the words suggesting a mixture of light and dark strike me as one-word poems. Gerard Manley Hopkins called his great lyric about dappled things 'Pied Beauty,' and to my ear such adjectives — and the condition they describe — seem homey, down to earth, essentially human. Nothing in our lives is pure and unalloyed; we love and we hate simultaneously, we act well and badly from one moment to the next. Our very souls are pieced together like old quilts or rag rugs."

That last sentence is rather poetic, if I do say so myself. I now wonder if I was overstraining for effect.

Anyone who writes a lot eventually develops, then starts to overuse, certain "fallback" words. When I want an intensifier I often resort to "wonderfully," as in "wonderfully inventive." One of my fellow journalists struggles against over-using the phrase "That said" as a convenient way to transition into a new paragraph. When "embonpoint" appeared in one of my book reviews, it was passed over in silence; when it showed up again a week later, my colleagues never let me forget it. "Look at his embonpoint! Did you ever see such embonpoint? I'm not fat, I just have a lot of embonpoint." I don't think I've ever used the word since.

Still, I do turn to my thesaurus more and more these days. As my style leans toward the ascetically austere, I really do need the occasional striking word to give it a bit of pizzazz. Or do I mean razzledazzle? Or . . . You see what I mean.

In the past, the devout or the well educated would often retire for the evening with their Bible, the plays of Shakespeare, or similar improving works. The novelist Patricia Highsmith later adopted this same practice, but she read the dictionary for half an hour after dinner. Sometimes I've wondered if even Hamlet might have been brushing up on his Elizabethan, thesaurus in hand, when Polonius asked him what he was reading and he answered: "Words, words, words."

Maybe I should emulate the noble prince's

example. (How quickly fancies become facts!) Settle down in the evening with my trusty *Oxford American Writer's Thesaurus*. Memorize a slew of new adjectives. Build up the old vocabulary. But somehow all this sounds more than a little pathetic. For now, at least, I think I'd prefer to spend the early evening with a glass of wine. Or since summer is fast upon us, a cold bottle of beer. Maybe two.

COWBOYS AND CLUBMEN

During most of my life I've thought of myself as a loner, an unexpected consequence of watching far too many westerns on Saturday afternoons when young. Alas, I never quite managed to become a drifter, the easygoing kind who moseys into the sunset as the credits roll. But even now I keep on my desk a silverplated cap gun used throughout my childhood in innumerable games of Cowboys and Indians. The trigger still has a nice feel to it — I've just fired off a couple of quick shots, which I sometimes do when frustrated by a piece of writing. No caps, though. They would frighten Cinnamon, the wonder cat of Silver Spring, Maryland.

For good or ill, my ideal of masculine comportment derives from movies and TV shows about strangers who ride into town, don't say much about themselves, and inevitably turn out to be the fastest guns alive. Indeed, I remember an old Glenn Ford film with just that title: *The Fastest Gun Alive.* If I recall correctly, at one point somebody extends his arm and drops a silver dollar. Before it hits the ground, Glenn has drawn his sidearm and put a bullet hole smack in the center of the coin.

Despite many years in which I secretly imagined myself as James Coburn in *The Magnificent Seven* or as the equally taciturn Clint Eastwood in *A Fistful of Dollars,* I've recently come to recognize that I've been living a lie. How can you think of yourself as a black-garbed "knight without armor in a savage land," as Richard Boone was called in *Have Gun, Will Travel,* if, in fact, you belong to a dozen social organizations and dining clubs? How frou-frou is that?

What's more, I'm a proud member of all of them. There's The Baker Street Irregulars, the nearly 80-year-old literary organization devoted to honoring Mr. Sherlock Holmes. Then there's Eta Sigma Phi, the national classical organization. My name also appears on the rosters of the North American Jules Verne Society, The Ghost Story Society, the Washington DC Panthans (devotees of Edgar Rice Burroughs) and the Lewis Carroll Society. After giving a talk last year at the Nebula Awards, I was tickled to be made an honorary member of the Science Fiction Writers of America. I attend, all too infrequently, meetings of Capital! Capital!, the local chapter of The P. G. Wodehouse Society. And just this spring I joined the Mystery Writers of America.

Twenty-five years ago I once even belonged to the exclusive Arthur Inman Society. Inman was a notorious recluse, who kept a voluminous diary, eventually edited by Daniel Aaron into two extremely thick volumes. The club comprised people, then living in Washington, who had actually read the diary. There was no other requirement. Besides me, the group included my late (and much-missed) *Washington Post* colleague Reid Beddow, the longtime *New Yorker* editor and novelist Jeffrey Frank, and the *Bangkok Post* columnist Bob Halliday.

As it happens, I also helped establish an even more chi-chi group: the Dawn Powell Society of Washington. It was founded in a bar when four journalists — all winners of a prize that starts with P — were sitting around drinking too much and talking about their shared admiration for the novelist Dawn Powell. I happened to have a copy of Powell's diaries with me, so on its endpapers I scribbled out the name of the organization, along with its board of directors.

Music critic Tim Page, novelist Lorraine Adams, *New Yorker* writer Kate Boo, and I all signed it. The DPSW, its members now long dispersed, has never met again.

But The League of Extraordinary Gentlemen is, happily, still going strong. This organization, it should be explained, facetiously adopted its grandiose name from Alan Moore's graphic novel, though such a self-designation isn't altogether inappropriate. The League's membership remains top secret, in part because it exercises immense power in our nation's capital, albeit from the wings, *sub rosa*. The current Gentlemen include two leading scientists for the Secret Service (one an expert on documents, the other on fingerprints), arguably the country's foremost forensic anthropologist, an authority on early cinema, a professor of classics, a distinguished science journalist, the director of African Studies at a major university, a freelance editor, a guy who has read every one of the 100 best books in the Western canon (not I), a leading scholar of the English Romantics, and our chief, the master of those who know or need to know — a former New Orleans private eye, now universally esteemed for his authorship of the standard guide to library research. Just as The Baker Street Irregulars reveres Sherlock, so the League pays homage to his smarter brother, Mycroft Holmes, who sometimes "*is* the British government."

Enough. I fear that all this talk of exclusive clubs and sodalities must sound elitist as all get out or at least a bit discomfiting. But let me add that there's one outstanding organization I don't belong to: Phi Beta Kappa, the organization that sponsors The American Scholar and, consequently, these essays. My first two years of college were — shall we say? — checkered. Still, I've always fancied owning a waistcoat from which one of those little keys would dangle on a thin gold chain. When people noticed me casually twirling it about, I would say, "This? Oh, it's just my Phi Beta Kappa key. Got it as a sophomore, don't you know? Something about mine being a special case. It was back about the time I won that chess championship and was elected president of Mensa. . . ."

Hmm. I think I'd better stick with the cowboy fantasy. The Hash Knife gang has been getting out of hand lately, threatening those sheepherders, the old marshal's taken to drink, and the good townfolk need serious help. Picture the pretty schoolmarm or the feisty dance hall girl — I can go either way on this — as she hurries to the telegraph office. In her gloved hand is a business card, and you can just make out a few words: Wire Paladin, Silver Spring, Maryland.

GRADES

The spring semester officially ended earlier this week at the University of Maryland. Last Sunday, May 20, under a perfect blue sky, seniors tossed their mortarboards into the air, then went on to open houses and lawn parties to celebrate. I confess that I can't help but envy all those smiling graduates just starting out in life, so full of youth and energy and dreams. When I look back. . . .

Stop. Let's not go further down that path toward corny commencement-style remarks, shall we? After all, my own thoughts on such occasions can generally be boiled down to: "Best of luck, kids. Have fun."

I filed the grades for my class on "The Modern Adventure Novel" last Friday. Setting aside the demands of marking 35 final exams and as many term papers in little more than a week, I would say that assigning grades is the worst part of being a teacher. Do you judge by performance and accomplishment alone? How important is effort or improvement? Should one err on the side of kindness — more grade inflation! — or insist on a return to standards, whatever those are?

In my own life, grades have always been a vexation. When I was very little, my report cards tended to be speckled with U's — for Unsatisfactory — or with hand-scrawled remarks saying "Needs Improvement." In high school I regularly flouted pedagogical authority, such that I would often receive shockingly poor marks. For the first grading period of my senior year, I earned — and let me stress that verb — a D in English. As for college: well, I struggled manfully for two years to break out of the category of the hardworking B-minus student. I did eventually, but by then the psychological damage was done.

At any given moment since, I've always assumed that nearly everyone around me was smarter than I was, more naturally gifted, quicker-witted, and probably capable of understanding Heidegger and Derrida. Even now people frequently snicker when I admit that I can't fathom what Wittgenstein meant by "The world is everything that is the case." They look pitying when I confess that all those "intuitive" aspects of digital technology aren't intuitive to me. Yes, with concerted effort I can follow written instructions, but don't ask me to simply grasp how to operate a smartphone. My own $20 Nokia from Radio Shack has features that even now remain mysterious to me. What, for instance, is a Media Net? Don't even start to explain. It won't mean anything to me.

No, long ago I realized that my only real talent can be reduced to a single word: doggedness. I'm sometimes willing to put in vast, even inordinate amounts of time if I find a project that interests me. I will then study with Talmudic devotion, consult experts, adopt training regimes that would inspire Olympians, and then, suddenly, drop whatever it is and move on. For years I ran or exercised every day and wore size 33 slacks. That's in the waist, not the length. Then, one day, I stopped, and now I'm embarrassed to get into my pajamas at night. My house itself is a shambles, being awash in vinyl LPs, classic men's clothing, manual typewriters, luggage of all kinds, scores of thrift-shop neckties and quite a few books. Okay, thousands of books. Many of them in boxes. In the basement. I've actually got six hulking double-sided bookcases, purchased from Borders when they went out of business, just sitting in my garage, waiting for a space to put them in. My wife draws the line at the dining room, even though we could easily eat our meals on trays.

People can be so judgmental too, and I have even heard words like "compulsive-obsessive" and "hoarding" spoken in my presence. That last sounds especially harsh. I really need all these heaped-up newspapers in the hallway. Okay, that was a joke, though I do have some pretty impressive stacks of old issues of the *Times Literary Supplement.* You never can tell when you'll want to settle down with an article about Roman coins of the fourth century.

Anyway, that's why I dislike grades. People are individual, so how can you reduce them to an A, a B, or a C? Or even, sometimes, to a D — along with an invitation to stop by for a quiet chat with Dr. Calta, the high school principal?

ANGLOPHILIA

In Richard Ford's new novel, *Canada,* a provincial hotel owner mingles one evening with his guests: "Remlinger had on the brown felt fedora he often wore, and one of his expensive Boston tweed suits that made him stand out strangely in the bar. His reading glasses were hung around his neck. He was wearing a bright red tie, and the tweed trousers were pushed down in the tops of his leather boots. I didn't know this at the time, but later I understood he was dressed like an English duke or baron who'd been out walking his estate and come in for a whiskey."

Like many Americans, I suffer from a mild case of Anglophilia, currently in higher gear than usual due to this week's celebration of Queen Elizabeth's 60-year jubilee. Since adolescence, I've frequently wondered, in the deepest chambers of my heart, whether my name might one day simply appear on her majesty's birthday honours list, pricked down for a knighthood or an OBE. And why not? I certainly spend enough time day-dreaming about wax cotton jackets from Barbour, Harrods picnic hampers, box seats at the Grand National and the Henley Regatta, and pub lunches of shepherd's pie and bitters. Nor should we overlook the reveries about pheasant hunting near Balmoral with my trusty Purdey shotgun, rainy Saturday afternoons at the Tate studying the Turners, chill evenings spent sipping single-malt Scotch whiskey at The George and Dragon, long autumn tramps through the Lake District or along the fells, and, of course, those riotous weekends at Oxford or Chatsworth with Evelyn, Cyril, Paddy, and all the Mitford sisters (even Jessica). To me at least, it really does seem a gross oversight that I never attended university at Cambridge or Edinburgh. As P. G. Wodehouse once said of Lord Ickenham, even now I retain the bright enthusiasms and the fresh, unspoiled mental outlook of a slightly inebriated undergraduate.

For the most part, though, my real-life Anglophilia is restricted to Harris Tweed sport coats, some Turnbull & Asser dress shirts, and a Burberry raincoat — all of them acquired at Amvets Value Village. Sometimes

I do watch aging VHS tapes of British television's Hercule Poirot and Miss Marple mysteries, less to guess the identity of the murderer than to look at the wonderful clothes and the idyllic Cotswoldian village of St. Mary Mead. My wife tells me I should check out *Downton Abbey,* but I gather that series might be almost too intense for my temperate nature.

In truth, my Anglophilia is fundamentally bookish: I yearn for one of those country house libraries, lined on three walls with mahogany bookshelves, their serried splendor interrupted only by enough space to display, above the fireplace, a pair of crossed swords or sculling oars and perhaps a portrait of some great English worthy. The fourth wall would, of course, open onto my gardens, designed and kept up by Christopher Lloyd, with the help of Robin Lane Fox, who would also be sure that there were occasional Roman antiquities — statues of nymphs and cupidons — along the graveled walks. The fountain itself — did I mention the fountain? — would center on a sculptural group showing Triton blowing his wreathèd horn, while various bare-breasted Nereids drape themselves in mute adoration around and across his rippling thighs.

But back to the library. It almost goes

without saying that the floor would be dark-stained wood, adorned with Persian carpets. Leather armchairs would butt up against the fender of the huge fireplace. On the long library table one would naturally find, neatly stacked, the current newspapers (*The Guardian, Le Monde*), old issues of *Horizon,* the *Times Literary Supplement* and *Country Life,* and a selection of literary and cultural periodicals from around the world. If I peer closely at the table through the haze — those applewood logs for the fire must have been wet — I can just make out several copies of *The American Scholar.*

I've never been quite sure whether to have an old wireless in one corner, or whether that properly belongs in the music room, along with my treasured vinyl LPs. Occasionally I do think about adding a Victorian card table for rubbers of bridge in the evening with my neighbors Doctor Hesselius, old Jorkens, and Brigadier Ffellowes (ret.). They've had some unusual experiences and each is always good for a story or two. There would definitely be a worn leather Chesterfield sofa, its back covered with a quilt (perhaps a tartan? decisions, decisions) and its corners cushioned with a half-dozen pillows embroidered with scenes from Greek mythology. Here, I would recline and read my books.

What books, you ask? Ah, now there I don't have to imagine. I may actually live in a pokey little brick colonial, its outside wood trim much in need of fresh paint, with an embarrassingly dilapidated kitchen, two bathrooms that were new about 1940, and closets designed by elves to hold no more than two shirts and a belt. But my library would fit right into my daydream. In fact, that's probably the only place it would fit, given that most of it now resides in boxes in the basement or locked away in a rented storage unit. I long ago ran out of bookshelf space and so, like a museum with its art, simply rotate my books from the boxes to the shelves and back again. Not that I enjoy doing this. Which is why I daydream about the baronial splendor of that country house library. It would gladden my aging heart to actually see all my books — most of them serious-looking hardbacks — arranged and displayed in substantial bookcases. And without being double-shelved.

But enough of this idle reverie. It's time to get on with the day. First, I need to go over the field accounts with my new game-keeper, a highly energetic chap by the name of Mellors. Can't imagine why old Chatterley let him go.

AFTER THE GOLDEN AGE

All of us remember the favorite books of our childhoods. That's when stories affect us most, giving us a glimpse of the world beyond our bedroom walls or presenting various options for the kind of life we might aspire to. As a boy, I frequently reflected on the respective merits of becoming a dashing riverboat gambler, professional private eye, or treasure-seeking pirate. There was always a lot of money in these reveries, and, as I grew a bit older, a number of slinkily attired women too. These last often resembled certain female classmates of mine, except that the silken dream lovelies, unlike the classmates, actually seemed interested in me.

As a young reader, I particularly loved boys' adventure books and comics. Certain names are holy even now: Uncle Scrooge, Tarzan, Sherlock Holmes, Rick Brant and Ken Holt, Green Lantern, The Flash, Jules

Verne, The Hardy Boys, Dr. Fu Manchu, Robert A. Heinlein, H. P. Lovecraft, Lord Dunsany. We never do read again with that wonderful, breathless excitement that is ours at 14, the Golden Age of Science Fiction, Mystery, and Romance. Or do we?

I was thinking back recently to some of the books I discovered in later years, at college and in my twenties, that do seem to me comparably life-changing. We should, I suspect, be vigilant in over-mythologizing early reading at the expense of later, more grown-up books. As Randall Jarrell pointed out, in all those Golden Ages people actually complained about how yellow everything was.

In college, for instance, I was idly wandering through Oberlin's co-op bookstore one afternoon when I noticed a paperback with a big number 7 on an otherwise white cover. I picked it up and began to read William Empson's *Seven Types of Ambiguity.* The book came as a revelation: Beneath the surface of even the simplest-seeming poem, I learned, there crackled unsuspected energies, connections, and meanings. The scales dropped from my eyes and suddenly I could *see* poetry.

As a junior I enrolled in a one-semester French course devoted to reading, in its entirety, Proust's *À la recherche du temps perdu.* Our teacher, Vinio Rossi, doubtless underestimated the time it would take for 20-year-olds to work their way through three thick Pléiade volumes. But I was enchanted by the classic simplicity of that well known opening line — *"Longtemps, je me suis couché de bonne heure"* ("For a long time I went to sleep early") — and completely seduced by the languorous beauty of Proustian prose. Most of all, though, the almost stand-alone novella, *Un Amour de Swann (Swann in Love),* seemed written for me. Is there a better account in literature of sexual enthrallment? I was then madly infatuated with a Titian-haired beauty who seemed a lot like Odette de Crécy. I, too, knew the racking torments of jealousy and possessiveness. In the end, of course, Swann recognizes that he had spent years of his life, even wanted to die, because of a woman who was, he finally realizes, "not my type at all."

During my early years in graduate school, my main interest was medieval literature. Which explains why, in a happy moment, I signed up for a course on the Icelandic saga. I didn't really know much about Northern Literature, which I then basically associated with myths about Loki and Thor, marauding Vikings, and Wagner's *Ring* cycle. But the *Laxdaela Saga, Grettir's Saga,* and *Njál Saga* swept me back into a world of adventure not unlike that of Sergio Leone's spaghetti westerns, only with swords, in the winter, on ice. The foster son of Njál, the lone survivor of a massacre, methodically tracks down the 40 men responsible for the destruction of the only family he has ever known. Cursed by a demon, Grettir — the strongest warrior in Iceland — suddenly finds himself afraid of the dark. I soon read every saga I could find, and there are quite a few of them. A hefty one-volume compilation is *The Sagas of Icelanders,* with a preface by novelist and fellow fan Jane Smiley.

In graduate school I also discovered that certain scholarly books could produce an intellectual exhilaration that rivaled the more visceral thrills of childhood reading. Erich Auerbach's *Mimesis: The Representation of Reality in Western Literature* made me wish to become an erudite, multilingual, European polymath. I soon realized that was never going to happen, though one could still, in a small, provincial way, try. Peter Brown's *Augustine of Hippo* brought the fourth century and its philosophical crosscurrents to blazing life. We all know about young Augie's famous plea, "Lord, make me chaste, but not yet." What Brown's book does, however, is reveal the astonishing evolution of that capacious, world-altering intellect, and he makes it an unputdownable page-turner. Because of *Augustine of Hippo,* late antiquity came to seem as exciting, as revolutionary and ideologically riven, as the 1960s.

In fact, for a long time biographies and autobiographical books replaced novels as my favorite genre. Rousseau's *Confessions* bewitched me away with its limpid prose-poetry, and I've never forgotten many of its episodes, in particular the evening Jean-Jacques entertains a celebrated Venetian courtesan. When this toast of the canals disrobes, he notices a small blemish on her breast and slightly recoils. Immediately, she gathers up her clothes and sweeps out the door, brusquely dismissing Rousseau with the phrase, *"Lascia le donne e studia la matematica!"* — "Give up women and study mathematics!"

In my late 20s, I devoured Richard Ellmann's *James Joyce,* the portrait of the modernist as a literary saint, Rupert Hart-Davis's underappreciated *Hugh Walpole,* a stunning depiction of an ambitious young writer on the make during the early 20th century, and S. Schoenbaum's *Shakespeare's Lives,* which tracks the multiple ways we have imagined and distorted the biography of our greatest playwright. All these were utterly riveting, and remain among my favorite books to this day.

In my 30s and after, the books that seemed to catch me at the heart or change my inner life grew fewer, but there are at least a dozen — Gilbert Sorrentino's *Imaginative Qualities of Actual Things,* for instance, and Casanova's exhilarating memoirs. But they will keep for another day, another column.

According to Longfellow, a boy's will is the wind's will, and the thoughts of youth are long, long thoughts. Sometimes very long. So even now I still keep a deck of cards at my desk and sometimes practice dealing seconds. There's a rumpled trench coat in the closet, and I'm on my guard around dames named O'Shaughnessy. Not least, I've made sure that there's a black flag displaying the skull and crossbones neatly packed away in a dresser drawer, just beneath my old French mariner's sweater. Who knows? Someday, yet, I may still hoist the Jolly Roger.

ANTHOLOGIES
AND COLLECTIONS

As a kid, I loved anthologies, all those fat volumes with titles like *The Golden Argosy, Great Tales of Terror and the Supernatural, Reading I've Liked, Ghostly Tales to Be Told, The Omnibus of Crime.* Some of these tomes — several ran to 700 or more pages — I would check out from the library and devour, story after story, over the course of the allotted three weeks; others I might discover at a thrift shop and take home for a dime or a quarter and then just dip into from time to time. In the cellars of a few of my relatives one could even find old Literary Guild and Book-of-the-Month Club volumes, with titles like *Stories to Remember* or *A Treasury of Great Mysteries,* each edited by a literary eminence of the day — Clifton Fadiman, Howard Haycraft, Bennett Cerf, John Beecroft, or the novelists Ellery Queen and Thomas B. Costain. I'd borrow these from my cousin Marlene or Aunt Stella, and sometimes I'd give them back.

In those days an author's name meant almost nothing to me. Who were W. W. Jacobs and Ambrose Bierce? Charlotte Perkins Gilman and Richard Connell? E. M. Forster and Anthony Berkeley and Shirley Jackson? I hadn't a clue. What mattered were those evocative titles: "The Monkey's Paw," "An Occurrence at Owl Creek Bridge," "The Yellow Wallpaper," "The Most Dangerous Game," "The Other Side of the Hedge," "The Avenging Chance," "The Lottery."

So it was that during my adolescence I was gradually introduced to the classics of short fiction, in nearly all the genres. I'll never forget the first time I read the late Ray Bradbury's "Zero Hour" in an author's choice volume called *My Best Science Fiction Story.* Bradbury's wonderful conceit — spoiler alert! — is that aliens secretly persuade children to play a game called Invasion. On the last page a little girl skips lightly up the stairs of her house, followed by the heavier trudge of Something behind her, and opens the door to where her terrified parents are hiding — at which point Bradbury brings this macabre miniature to its perfect and chilling close, as the child murmurs: "Peekaboo."

Throughout adolescence I sought out all

sorts of storytelling showcases. In *The Science Fiction Hall of Fame,* edited by Robert Silverberg, I first read Cordwainer Smith's "Scanners Live in Vain" — note, again, that haunting title — and the heartbreaking "Flowers for Algernon" by Daniel Keyes. Alfred Hitchcock anthologies such as *Stories That Scared Even Me, Stories for Late at Night* and *Stories to be Read with the Door Locked* introduced me to myriad chillers and thrillers, including that tour de force of logical deduction, Harry Kemelman's "The Nine Mile Walk" and Jack Finney's unnerving "I'm Scared." (The versatile Finney's novels include that classic of 1950s paranoia, *The Body Snatchers,* and the most romantic of all time travel stories, *Time and Again.*) In more general anthologies I discovered work by other great practitioners of commercial short fiction: O. Henry, Somerset Maugham, Irwin Shaw, and John Cheever, as well as modern mini-classics by such literary folk as Maupassant, Chekhov, Katherine Mansfield, and Frank O'Connor.

Today, though, I hardly ever pick up an anthology. At some point, I realized that I had grown more interested in collections, that is, volumes of stories gathering the work of a single author. Rather than read just one of Lord Dunsany's tall tales about

Joseph Jorkens, or one of Robert Aickman's "strange stories," or one of P. G. Wodehouse's misadventures of Jeeves and Wooster, I found that I wanted to read them all. Or at least a lot of them. What attracts me these days aren't short fiction's high-spots so much as an individual writer's overall voice and style, the atmosphere he or she creates on the page. I want to immerse myself in an entire oeuvre rather than flit from one short masterpiece to another.

In effect, anthologies resemble dating. You enjoy some swell times and suffer through some awful ones, until one happy hour you encounter a story you really, really like and decide to settle down for a while with its author. Of course, this doesn't lead to strict fidelity, except in the cases of fans who spend their entire lives researching and obsessing about, say, Arthur Conan Doyle or H. P. Lovecraft. Rather, one adopts a pattern of serial monogamy. Weeks go by or even months, as you read *The Collected Stories of Eudora Welty,* but inevitably there comes a day when you decide you just can't face another page about the inhabitants of Morgana, Mississippi, and you find yourself suddenly, irresistibly attracted to James Salter or Sarah Orne Jewett or Alice Munro. Your friends may shake their heads over the break-up — you were so crazy about "A Worn Path" and "Why I Live at the P. O." — but still, it's the modern world, what can you say, these things happen. Besides, more often than not, after a few mad, wonderful weeks or months with J.G. Ballard or Robert Aickman you'll find yourself remembering "The Petrified Man" or "No Place for You, My Love," and then one evening you'll be standing at Eudora's front door. This being literature, not life, she'll take you back without a word.

Rocky Mountain Low

There's an old saying — adopted by Leonard Woolf as the title for one of his volumes of autobiography — that "the journey not the arrival matters." There's also an old slogan — first used by Cunard ocean liners — that enthusiastically proclaimed that "getting there is half the fun." Obviously neither Virginia Woolf's husband nor the elegant passengers of the *QE II* ever tried to go hiking in Rocky Mountain National Park in June 2012.

Let me point out, before I begin my apoplectic rant, that once upon a time I viewed myself as a resourceful and easygoing traveler. At the age of 14 I ran away from home for four days and hitchhiked around western Pennsylvania and southern Ohio. At 17 I traveled to Mexico in a lemon yellow Mustang and saved money by bunking down in cheap, cockroach-infested flophouses. Great times both. In my early 20s I went on to thumb rides through Europe, readily sleeping in train stations, my backpack as a pillow. Once I even hunkered down for a night on a sidewalk grate — for warmth — in Paris.

Somehow travel was an adventure then, not simply an endurance test. In the early 1970s my parents dressed up in their Sunday best — my father in coat and tie, my mother in a severe gray outfit — to take the Greyhound Bus from Lorain, Ohio, to Ithaca, New York. I remember when riding the train still felt, just a little, like an adventure on the Orient Express, and when TWA might hand out free flight bags, and canapes would be served by a uniformed stewardess, and when you could count on a knowledgeable travel agent to advise you about trains and planes and hotels in far-off places.

Gone, all gone.

Today, we expect travel to be a prolonged nightmare. And it is. You spend hours online searching for a cheap flight, then discover that your air miles have all expired. Ever worsening traffic jams slow your rush to the airport. Pause too long at dropoff or pickup, and police shout at you to move along. Inside the terminal, pythonesque lines snake their way slowly toward the distant security checkpoint. You feel hot, your luggage is heavy, you wonder if you'll miss the plane. Eventually, you find yourself disrobing in public, removing your shoes, coat, belt, watch, cellphone, laptop, and pocket change while the people behind you grow restless, wishing you would hurry up. TSA agents pounce on your normal-sized can of shaving cream and ask, "Is this yours?" Out it goes. The X-ray machine, or sometimes a gloved official, intimately examines your body in all its flabby glory. Finally, you rush to repack all your items and relace your shoes, before discovering that the scheduled flight has been delayed for 20 minutes, 45 minutes, three hours, and finally canceled because of bad weather in Chicago. If you do board, tension mounts and tempers flare as the overhead luggage racks fill up because no one wants to pay extra to check a suitcase or risk losing one. Finally, when you settle into a middle seat just in front of the back lavatory, stressed and hungry, the only food available arrives in cellophane snack-packs, and . . .

But why go on? We all know these horrors. Every time I see the crowds inching their way forward toward ticket counters, through airport security, or at boarding gates the same line from *The Waste Land* goes through my head: "I had not thought that death had undone so many."

Anyway, a little more than 10 days ago I found myself in Colorado for a wedding, in company with my Beloved Spouse, and my Number 1 and Number 2 Sons, along with their respective girlfriends. (Son number 3 remained at home, theoretically minding the house but actually throwing three parties in a single week, one of said parties being announced on Facebook, along with an open invitation to any roaming barbarian hordes to stop by if they and their fellow Visigoths had nothing better penciled in on their dance cards.)

Meanwhile, in Evergreen, Colorado, the bride and groom celebrated their nuptials at a rustic inn, the drink flowed, and a good time was had by all, even if far too much hip-hop music was played to the neglect of the "Beer Barrel Polka" and the golden oldies of the 1960s, back when rock was young.

After the festivities, my eldest son returned to his studies in Denver, my middle son flew back to his job in New York, and their onlie begetters — those poor lost souls — set off for a day's hiking in the Rocky Mountains. To begin our excursion Beloved Spouse and I drove our rental car up to Estes Park, a town of motels, boutiques, and restaurants, best known as the location of that imposing compound called The Stanley Hotel, the inspiration for Stephen King's *The Shining* — and an obvious sign to all sensible people to turn back before it was too late. To paraphrase Thomas Gray: alas, regardless of their doom, the latest victims play!

The evening before our much anticipated day of communing with the Colorado sublime we stopped for soup and salad at The Baldpate Inn. En route to Estes Park I had noticed its sign, paused briefly to wonder, then wondered even further when I observed the picture of a gigantic key underneath the inn's name. Could this possibly be the inspiration for the once famous mystery novel, *Seven Keys to Baldpate,* written by Earl Derr Biggers some years before he created his famous detective Charlie Chan? In fact, the charming hostelry was established in 1917 and took its name from the novel, with Biggers's blessing. Over the years since, the Baldpate Inn had gradually created a museum of keys from around the world, including one to the room where Edgar Allan Poe lodged at the University of Virginia. Yet while the darkness fell and Mr. and Mrs. Dirda innocently enjoyed their dinner, little did they know, as old mystery novels used to say, of the horror that awaited them the following morning and afternoon.

The next day at 9:30 A.M. the doomed couple left their rented Impala at the Estes Park Visitors Center, having been informed that there was construction on the road into Rocky Mountain National Park. Cars were prohibited from entering after 9 A.M., and visitors were required to take a shuttle bus to a ranger station, where they would then change to a second bus that would carry them to the various trailheads. Nothing was said about any serious delays. One imagined a flagman in a hardhat, perhaps a five-minute wait, traffic alternating through the usual single lane around the work zone.

The day was hot, the bus crowded and without air conditioning. We waited for half an hour at the construction site before we finally got through. Then, as we pulled into the ranger station, each passenger stared with disbelief at a line a block long, where — we soon learned — people had already been standing for 45 minutes in the now vicious sun, patiently or restlessly awaiting the arrival of the second bus, the one that would take them to the trails. When one such vehicle finally appeared, it absorbed 40 or 50 people, then tootled merrily away. The line hardly seemed to have shrunk. When another bus finally appeared, we were lucky to make the cut for standing room. It took off, then halted at a second construction site where another half hour went by. It took us more than two hours to travel a few miles just to begin our John Muir–like saunter through the scrub and scrim up to three mountain lakes.

The next couple of hours were lovely, despite our gasping for oxygen in the higher altitudes, and we even saw a bluejay, a bird I hadn't glimpsed since my childhood. And an elk. And lots of impressive rocks, cliffs, and torrents, as well as snow in summer. Unfortunately, we'd been in such a rush to get going early — ha! — that we'd only brought a bag of raisins and nuts. Naturally, the ranger station and trailhead stocked maps and souvenir lanyards, but nothing whatsoever to eat.

We returned then, ravenous, at 2:20 to start our trip back to our parked rental car. Surely the travel situation couldn't be any worse. What naivete! Is this America or what? This time our bus journey took a purgatorial three hours. We waited again in the sun for the first bus; after an hour it dawdled in and conveyed a tired crowd to the ranger station, where we expected to see the second bus. A child would have been less credulous. Because of the growing crowd, the rangers had divided people up into groups and ours — those who had parked in town, rather than at one of the other car-sites — was shunted to a separate line where we waited and waited and waited. Eventually, in a controlled fury that Christopher Marlowe's Tamburlaine might have learned from, I told the local ranger that such abuse of the park's visitors was cruel, insulting and intolerable. She agreed with me and shrugged. When the second bus finally arrived, we wearily climbed on and journeyed 10 minutes down the rutted road, at which point the vehicle, overloaded with tired, desperate people, broke down. We waited for a third rescue bus, forbidden from leaving the one in which we were slowly cooking. People began to grow hysterical.

Somehow, we eventually reached the parking lot of the Visitors Center, but only after many passengers had been dropped off at two intervening parking areas. By now it was 5:30 in the afternoon. Our original plans were ruined. For a couple of hours of hiking we had spent most of the day on a bus or waiting for one.

Calming myself — no mean feat — I approached the main desk inside the Visitors' Center, gently pointed out that the actual road conditions and traffic delays were of an order of magnitude quite unlike that suggested by their sparky staff, then strongly underscored the real suffering of elderly seniors and quite young children, and finally suggested they tell people the truth and send them to other entrances to the park. Naturally, the Center's personnel regarded me as a pitiable crank and dismissed my outrage as obvious insanity. But here is the strangest part of all: no one else came forth to utter a peep about our cattle-car experiences. I was shocked at how docile my fellow sufferers had become. Were they too beaten down to say anything? Had they come to accept such abusive behavior as the *modus operandi* for life in these United States?

Perhaps some readers will regard all this as trivial. I can see that. I mean, we have real crises with unemployment, health care, terrorism, crumbling economies around the world. Nonetheless, my experiences strike me as still another sign that those in power, whether it be corporate or governmental, have grown increasingly disconnected, increasingly callous in their treatment and exploitation of ordinary Americans. I once thought the part of me that, years ago, joined the Students for a Democratic Society was dead. Not entirely. I still feel outrage. Somehow, big banks lose billions and wreck people's savings and retirement accounts, yet their plutocrat executives still take home obscene bonuses. You don't have to be an economics major to recognize that something here does not compute.

Oh, well, that Dirda! He's just a literary guy, head in the clouds and all, no real understanding that everything is for the best in this best of all possible countries. Better he should stick to writing about books. Maybe so. But I won't be visiting the Rockies at Estes Park again. Nor should you. My one vacation day in beautiful Colorado wasn't entirely wrecked — those mountains are glorious — but I was left angry and depressed that in the midst of nature I couldn't escape governmental indifference and bureaucratic ineptitude, or the overwhelming sense that I wasn't being viewed as a human being but only as a statistic, a number, a vote, a cash cow. Leonard Woolf, I should point out, titled another volume of his autobiography *Downhill All the Way.*

THE FUGITIVE

Fans of the old television show *The Fugitive* may remember the striking sequence that opened each episode. First we glimpse a man, handcuffed, sitting on a train, just staring out the window, and then we hear the portentous voiceover: "Richard Kimble looks out on the world for the last time and sees only darkness." Pause. "But in that darkness Fate moves its huge hand." At which point the train loudly crashes, and in the next scene Kimble is running through the underbrush, then stumbling and falling into some muddy water, still manacled, as the words "The Fugitive" flash across the family's black-and-white Sylvania TV screen.

Anyway, that's how I remember it, though I may be wrong on a few details.

This opening, repeated week after week, came to mind as I recently dipped into *The Fortunes of Permanence,* an exceptional new volume of essays by the editor/publisher of *The New Criterion.* Change but a word or two, *et voilà:* "Roger Kimball looks out on the world and sees only darkness. But in that darkness Fate moves its huge hand." Certainly, this eminent conservative intellectual perceives our country as assailed from without by fanatics, but more seriously corrupted from within by political and cultural relativism. And he clearly hopes for a miraculous return to sanity, repeatedly stressing in his work the established principles of western morality, the necessity of standards, and the bulwark and safeguard of tradition.

What interests me about Kimball isn't whether he is right or not about most political issues. Drawing on a capacious intelligence and a flair for the well-chosen quotation, he is an expert and often convincing polemicist. Nonetheless, he regularly exhibits the slash-and-burn zeal of a high-school debate champion, always going for the kill, seldom allowing for nuance or reservation or uncertainty. Just say the word "Obama," for instance, and he grows apoplectic.

But Roger Kimball is, whatever else he might be, a man of principle. I say this, even while acknowledging that my own political beliefs are utterly simple and may be reduced to a few shocking words: Listen to the young. Those under 30 see the inequities of the world and are willing to challenge the status quo. Fathers and mothers of families seldom rock the boat; they can't afford to risk losing what they have. Kimball would interject, Thank heaven for that saving grace.

Still, when it comes to education, literature, and art, Kimball strikes me as a model of good sense. This is troubling: if our tastes are so often congruent in cultural matters, perhaps I need to reexamine my supposed political convictions more closely? In *The Fortunes of Permanence,* for instance, Kimball reprints essays in defense of John Buchan, Rudyard Kipling, and G. K. Chesterton — three of my favorite writers, all of them now frequently derided as jingoist, imperialist and racist. Any good reader must instinctively loathe the kind of reductionist presentism and ethnocentrism that condescends to such great storytellers and artists, or that disses a magnificent book like *Kim* as a collection of western prejudices. Such knee-jerk attitudes, as Kimball writes, aim "to short-circuit, not refine, our powers of discrimination."

Because I admire the cultural coverage of *The New Criterion,* I've twice written for the magazine, once on the poetry of Stephen Crane and this spring on the work of Philip Larkin. The kind invitations to do so came from the executive editor and poet David Yezzi, who is now researching a biography of Anthony Hecht, one of the finest American poets of our time (as well as a man I counted as a friend). Indeed, nearly all the magazine's reviewing — of books, art, and music — is first-rate. The poetry featured is comparably exceptional, with a strong preference for formal verse (which is just fine by me). Nonetheless, I still frequently bristle and groan at the political and editorial snarkiness at the front of the book and in some of its columns.

In his famous elegy for W. B. Yeats, Auden said that, despite Yeats's various forms of foolishness, Time would pardon him for writing well. I tend to feel that way about many of the literary controversialists of our time, whether Christopher Hitchens, William F. Buckley, Mark Steyn, Gore Vidal, Nat Hentoff, or Roger Kimball. Of course, Auden also sternly warned against those who read the Bible not for its message but only for the beauty of its prose.

All these disparate journalists, it is clear, possess a formidable self-confidence, sometimes verging on smugness. There's nothing pallid or wishy-washy about them or their views. And perhaps just because of this they all produce (or produced) exhilarating essays and articles — even when they really do Go Too Far. But, as the French say, they also give you furiously to think.

Sigh. I myself sometimes wish that I could be as sure of anything as many writers seem to be about everything. But then I am burdened by having taken to heart, long ago, Cromwell's immortal reply to the Church of Scotland: "I beseech you, in the bowels of Christ, think it possible you may be mistaken." Not really the ideal motto for a critic, but there you are.

HOT ENOUGH FOR YOU?

So I'm sitting here, in the dark, at 10 P.M. on July 2, 2012, of the Common Era, sweating and thinking evil thoughts about the upper management of Pepco. For those of you who don't live in the so-called greater Washington, D.C., area, Pepco is the Potomac Electric Power Company. Three days ago a violent storm stomped D.C., Maryland, and Virginia and wreaked havoc, knocking over trees and telephone poles, leaving hundreds of thousands of people without electricity.

I, needless to say, am one of those hundreds of thousands.

From the moment the winds died down Pepco immediately began to "assess" the devastation and announced that it would be a week, or possibly more, before power was restored to everyone. Now, I dislike being without electricity as much as the next man or woman, but it's not as though this outage was something unprecedented or totally unique, once in a lifetime, never to be repeated. Every year, in summer or winter, the same thing happens — storms hit, followed by days without electricity — and I'm really tired of it.

Over the past weekend, with temperatures reaching the 100 degree mark, you couldn't sell your soul for a hunk of dry ice. I know because I tried. As a result, the Dirdas — and many, many other people — have had to throw out a huge quantity of good and costly food. Since last Friday night it's been impossible to work at my desk — i.e., to earn money to pay my bills, including the one from Pepco, which naturally instituted a rate increase on July 1 — because my home has become the kind of hothouse that the orchid-growing Nero Wolfe could only dream about. Not least, my beloved books, stored in the basement because there is no other place for them, are growing spongy and mildewy and could well be irrevocably ruined unless the dehumidifier starts running again soon. I know this because 30 years ago I wrote a little monograph called *Caring For Your Books*. Though I wouldn't go so far as to say that my library — a mere agglomeration of pulp, glue, and ink — means more to me than living, breathing human beings, it's a near thing. I'd certainly rescue the baby, not the *Mona Lisa,* from a burning house. But that baby had better grow up to find the cure for cancer. . . .

It's now two powerless days later, Wednesday, the Fourth of July, and my evil thoughts about Pepco haven't grown any more benign or forgiving. Are its overpaid corporate officers suffering in this record-setting Washington heat and humidity? Have *they* thrown out good food? Are their possessions growing mildew? Somehow I don't think so. Talk to almost anyone "served" — laughable word — by this apparently inept company and you'll discover the same disdain. Even the Maryland regulators admit that Pepco has failed to keep to proper standards (see the front page of *The Washington Post,* July 4). I remember an earlier *Post* article that pointed out that this company had one of the worst, or possibly *the* worst, service record, and the highest rates, for any comparable public utility in the country.

Okay. You'll say that's just the heat talking or that Dirda — once known as Mr. Sweetness and Light — has inherited the curmudgeonly persona formerly owned by his friend and *Book World* colleague Jon Yardley, who has, in his turn, now become a Grand Old Man of Letters (albeit one in terrific shape). Perhaps. But Cossack blood runs in my half-clogged veins, and I don't take well to excessive heat. Fortunately, this is only an early July heat and not "August heat" — those who remember W. F. Harvey's classic short story of that title will know what relentlessly high temperatures can lead to.

Fact is most stories about high temperatures lead to violence. There's the blazing Algerian sun of Albert Camus's *The Stranger,* and the long hot summers in Faulkner stories that culminate in rape and lynching, and all those "hot Santa Anas" you get in Raymond Chandler murder mysteries, and the kind of psychologically debilitating oppressiveness that Mr. Kurtz contended with, rather unsuccessfully, in *Heart of Darkness.* Then, too, one mustn't overlook my favorite science fiction short story, Alfred Bester's "Fondly Fahrenheit" — a dazzling tale of a robot and his master, of schizophrenia and murder: "It's no feat to beat the heat, all reet, all reet!"

But let's not veer too far away from Pepco, which I just realized is the kind of name you might find in a 1950s science fiction novel. In a just world, in an honorable world, the men and women who run this company would voluntarily go without electricity until they had restored power to everyone they "served." But given the slowness of the restoration, I suspect that Pepco has adopted Milton's motto: "They also serve who only stand and wait." Not that I blame the linemen and the workers out on the streets, who are doing their best: they're only human. I'm not so sure about their bosses. At all events, I picture the company's officers lounging in their air-conditioned great rooms, watching DVDs of *Lawrence of Arabia,* answering email, listening to hot jazz on their stereo systems, and sipping cold beers, in cool and beautiful comfort, probably even putting on a sweater vest against the AC chill.

Years ago, my steelworker father — a lifelong Democrat — announced that he would be voting for our hometown's Republican candidate for mayor, a fellow by the name of Woody Mathna. Being taken aback at this shocking news, I naturally asked why. Dad answered, "Mathna lives in our precinct." I wasn't smart enough to know what that meant. My father, shaking his head yet again over his idiot-child, said, "That means that when it snows the streets around Mathna's house will be plowed first. And ours will be one of them." All politics is local, sometimes very local, and *Realpolitik* is the most local of all.

Oh, well. As my father also solemnly used to say: this too shall pass. A fount of wisdom, my Dad. During my college years he would regularly intone, "Kid, I want you to get rich, have a house on a hill, drive a Cadillac, forget about stupid workingmen like me, and become a Republican." Sigh. I loved my father but, like sons everywhere, I never listened to him.

Last week I ranted about what it was like to live without electricity on five successive days of temperatures in the high 90s, in a house where most of the windows don't open. What I didn't mention was how I managed to get through one of those days, specifically Sunday, July 1, when almost everything in the immediate Washington area was closed because of downed power lines. The places shuttered included the Silver Spring and Wheaton libraries, the Glenwood swimming pool, and most of the local stores. After a 100 degree Saturday, I was desperate to find somewhere cool, somewhere I might take my mind off this latest outage — I almost typed *outrage* — as well as the prospect of days without refrigeration, lights, and air-conditioning.

So naturally, I turned my attention to the north, to Frederick, Maryland, to be more precise, about an hour away up I-270. Driving my beloved 1997 Maxima, which is much in need of a new muffler and which I really should get rid of, I gradually made my way to Wonder Book and Video.

Wonder Book's Frederick store is but one outlet of Chuck Roberts's used-book empire, rivaled in the greater Washington area only by Allan Stypeck's Second Story Books. But Second Story's Rockville warehouse is relatively nearby, so I generally drop by there every month or so. Frederick, by contrast, is a bit of a trip. Yet given that I had no power and, just as important, given that my Beloved Spouse was out of the country, I really had no choice but to spend the day in Frederick. I'm sure you can see that.

Also, because Chuck is a friend of mine, he offers me a discount, and because one has a discount, it seems only reasonable to buy more books than one might otherwise. At all events, I spent three hours going through the stock, stepped out for a quick bite at a fast-food joint, then spent another happy three hours before I called it a day. What did I acquire? I thought you'd never ask. In no particular order, I bought:

Tales of Mystery and Imagination, by Edgar Allan Poe, illustrated by Harry Clarke. This is a famous and highly desirable edition, but it was quite cheap because the volume, otherwise in very good condition, was missing three plates, including the frontispiece, as well as a page of text. Normally, I wouldn't look twice at such a damaged book, but it was still attractive just as a classic of bookmaking, and a fine, intact copy could cost several hundred dollars. Oddly enough, I'm not terribly bothered by its faults, given how beautiful it is overall.

The Long Ships, by Frans G. Bengtsson. Ever since I wrote an essay — for the online *Barnes and Noble Review* — pegged to the New York Review Classics paperback of this adventure novel, I've wanted to own a proper hardback. This copy's dust jacket has some losses to the spine and it's a second printing, but that's okay. I may even toss the dj. One of these days I'll spend a happy weekend rereading this exciting, and surprisingly witty saga of Viking exploits.

Startling Stories, November, 1950. This is a large-sized pulp magazine, printing in its entirety an early Jack Vance novel called *The Five Gold Bands.* Its cover features a Salome-like dancer being ogled by shady-looking aliens. Who could resist? Certainly no Vance fan, which I am, and have long been. Happily, my youngest son shares my passion for this greatest of all living science fiction and fantasy writers, so he may end up with the magazine as a Christmas present.

The Fools in Town Are on Our Side, by Ross Thomas. Years ago, I traded my mint first of this crime thriller to my friend David Streitfeld — and regretted it almost immediately. In my years as a book editor, I used to call up Ross Thomas to review mysteries and spy novels, and, a consummate professional, he was always at his desk. Like his contemporary Charles McCarry, happily still with us, Thomas never quite received the acclaim he deserved, though his fans are legion. In a *Times Literary Supplement* survey, of 25 years ago or more, Eric Ambler chose this novel as a neglected classic of its genre. The title, by the way, comes from *Huckleberry Finn.* Along with *Chinaman's Chance* and *The Seersucker Whipsaw,* both of which I've already read, *The Fools in Town Are on Our Side* is probably Thomas's most admired novel.

The Saturday Review of Literature, March 27, 1943. This special issue honors the memory of Stephen Vincent Benét, with contributions by his friends novelist Thornton Wilder, literary journalist Christopher Morley, playright Philip Barry, and many others. As I intend to write an essay on Benét's fantasy fiction — such stories as "The Devil and Daniel Webster" and "By the Rivers of Babylon" — this was an especially fortuitous find.

A Touch of Sturgeon, selected and introduced by David Pringle. This tight and handsome hardcover features eight stories by Theodore Sturgeon, arguably the greatest short-story writer in the history of American science fiction, especially if you assign Ray Bradbury to fantasy. Pringle, who is British, chooses almost all the most famous works, from "Killdozer" and "Mr. Costello, Hero" to "The Other Celia" and "Slow Sculpture." I've got paperbacks and a few hardbacks of pretty much Sturgeon's entire oeuvre (though not the multi-volume complete stories available to those with deeper pockets than mine). But for some reason, there in the store, I suddenly felt in the mood to reread some of his short fiction and I liked the heft and feel of this attractive hardback. By the way, Sturgeon's depiction of the mind of an idiot — in the opening section of his novel *More Than Human* — has always struck me as good as Faulkner's in the Benji section of *The Sound and the Fury.* Heresy, I know.

Riders in the Chariot, by Patrick White. I read half of this novel by Australia's Nobel Laureate years ago, but — unusually for me — put it aside and never went back to it. When I saw this pretty English first in a fine dj, I thought that I would give it another try.

Alfred Hitchcock Presents: Twelve Stories for Late at Night. This is just an ordinary paperback, but it contains many classic tales of science fiction and horror, including John Collier's "Evening Primrose," C. L. Moore's "Vintage Season," M. R. James's "The Ash-Tree," and Evelyn Waugh's "The Man Who Liked Dickens." I've enjoyed all these at one time or another. But this paperback also reprints Gouverneur Morris's "Back There in the Grass," which has been referred to as a classic lost-race story and the only thing the author is remembered for. Well, here was my chance to enjoy the story without shelling out serious money for Morris's scarce collection *It and Other Stories.* Morris did have a flair for titles — one of his other books is called *If You Touch Them They Vanish.*

The Silver Stallion, by James Branch Cabell. This is still another first edition, one of 850 signed and numbered large-paper copies, of arguably Cabell's best book. I first read it in the Ballantine Adult Fantasy series, edited by Lin Carter, but couldn't pass up a signed copy for only $4. Though his output is uneven, Cabell is probably the most significant American writer of ironic high fantasy. He is, of course, generally remembered for the once scandalous *Jurgen,* which was banned in Boston and championed by H. L. Mencken.

Short Talks with the Dead and Others, by Hilaire Belloc. Published in 1926, this is — as far as I can tell — a collection of casual essays, rebound in ugly library bookcloth. Belloc is under a cloud these days — he was, more or less, anti-Semitic — but he was also a consummate English prose stylist (and one of the first serious writers to acclaim the genius of P. G. Wodehouse). I own a number of Belloc's books, including *The Path to Rome,* and aim to read him at length one of these days.

The Murder League and *The Tricks of the*

Trade, both by Robert L. Fish. Being a member of The Baker Street Irregulars, I tend to look out for Sherlockian material. As all Irregulars know, few send-ups of the sacred canon are as hilarious as Robert L. Fish's *The Incredible Schlock Homes:* "To my mind, Watney, sabotage — next to the pilfering of coal — is the dirtiest of all crimes." But Fish also wrote several mystery and thriller series, which I've never read. *The Murder League* is about three aging crime novelists who form a kill-for-hire organization; *The Tricks of the Trade* is the first novel about Kek Huygens, the world's most successful smuggler. Needless to say, both books appear to share the lighthearted tone I favor in mysteries.

The Lunatic at Large, by J. Storer Clouston. Published in 1900 as part of Appleton's Town and Country Library, this is apparently the first American edition of a book reissued a few years back by McSweeney's. It's a comic novel, about, well, an escaped lunatic, an arranged marriage, and I don't know what else. Even though I possess the modern hardback, I always prefer to read books in their original editions whenever possible. Only those early formats possess the right feel, the right aura. Nonetheless, I won't pay a lot for a book I already own in a perfectly good edition — unless the price is right. This one was.

Dream Days, by Kenneth Grahame, illustrated by Maxfield Parrish. Published in 1902, this is the first illustrated edition of an early collection of stories — the best known being "The Reluctant Dragon" — by the author of *The Wind in the Willows.* It comes with a richly decorated cover showing a castle keep covered with shrubs, while the interior photogravure reproductions of Parrish's pictures represent the period's very latest in print technology. A very handsome book and greatly underpriced, probably because the copyright page makes clear that it's not the first printing. But that edition of 1898, which forgoes illustrations, is probably less desirable, at least for ordinary readers, than this one.

Mayfair, by Michael Arlen. This is a fine English 1925 first, in an Edmund Dulac jacket, of witty and cynical, and sometimes supernatural, stories, set among the bright young things of 1920s London. It includes the celebrated horror classic "The Gentleman from America." I've never read Arlen at length, and this seemed a golden opportunity to own a proper first of one of his best books. I already have a copy, not a first, of his most famous, or infamous novel, *The Green Hat.*

The Servant, by Robin Maugham. I bought this slender volume largely because of the striking and rather ominous cover design by G. N. Fish. I did know that the novella was the source of a celebrated Joseph Losey film, with a Harold Pinter screenplay, which I haven't seen. Years ago, however, I read Robin Maugham's two books about his uncle, Somerset Maugham, and liked them both. The nephew never quite emerged from the elder Maugham's shadow, but this novella, I suspect, will be a dark treat.

Well, I could go on and mention the copy of Hugh Lofting's *Doctor Doolittle in the Moon* (which, I failed to notice, offered some illustrations hand-colored by a juvenile artist of limited talent), or the copy of Nelson Bond's *Mr. Mergenthwirker's Lobblies and other Fantastic Tales,* in a water-damaged dust jacket, or the first paperback edition of Ray Bradbury's *The Martian Chronicles,* or the ex-library copy of Frederic Brown's *What Mad Universe* (albeit with a good dj).

I know, I know — I probably shouldn't

have bought quite so many books, or settled for several that are in rather shabby condition. Still, all my purchases were of works I love already or that I have long wanted to read. I'm no investor: I only collect books and authors I care about. When, that hot Sunday afternoon, I finally left Wonder Book and Video my wallet was certainly lighter than when I arrived, but then so was my heart.

READERCON

Every July for the past several years I've flown to Providence, Rhode Island, for a midsummer getaway from work and family. The focus of this long weekend is Readercon, a science fiction and fantasy convention held at a Marriott hotel in nearby Burlington, Massachusetts, about an hour's drive for one of my favorite couples, the writer and critic Paul Di Filippo and the knit-wear designer Deborah Newton.

A recent issue of *Locus,* the trade magazine of sf and fantasy, featured Paul on its cover, calling him the field's great "chameleon," the author of brilliantly imagined fiction, such as *The Steampunk Trilogy* (which popularized that term), *Roadside Bodhisattva,* and *A Princess of the Linear Jungle,* but also of humor pieces (some collected as *Plumage from Pegasus*), essays, serious reviews (many for a regular column for the online *Barnes and Noble Review*) and author profiles. His most recent book, written with Damien Broderick, is *Science Fiction: The 101 Best Novels, 1985–2010.*

Even Paul's envelopes and book mailers are distinctive, since he decorates them with gonzo collages, somewhat reminiscent of those of Max Ernst in *The Hundred Headless Women.* Paul once sent me a book in a large brown mailer, its outside cover enhanced with a large still from an episode of *I Love Lucy.* Sitting at her breakfast table, Lucy is reading *The Washington Post.* There's no trickery here. But Paul has inserted a thought balloon above Lucy's head that says: "I never understand anything that Michael Dirda writes." I look at this picture every day because, framed, it hangs above the bureau in my bedroom.

As for Deb: I once mentioned my friendship with her to one of our country's best poets, who reacted with something close to speechlessness. I actually *knew,* had spoken with, eaten meals with, clasped the knitting hand of Deborah Newton. You would have thought that I'd said I was a pal of Hillary Clinton or Angelina Jolie. I soon learned that if you murmur Deb's name to a serious knitter you should be prepared for a caesura of pure awe. Her books are knitting bibles.

146

When I travel to Providence, most years I join a number of other Di Filippo/Newton houseguests, usually including the SyFy Channel columnist Scott Edelman and writers Howard Waldrop and Michael Bishop. As you might guess, things grow maniacally festive even before we make the drive over to Burlington. But this year Mike couldn't get away, Howard decided to fly in through Boston, and Scott was obliged to report on Comic-Con, which was being held this same weekend in San Diego. Still, Scott did send a life-sized cardboard cutout of himself and Paul propped it up outside the main hall of the Marriott.

The first time I made this Readercon pilgrimage I insisted that Paul stop en route so that I could pay my respects at the grave of H. P. Lovecraft, who spent most of his 46 years in Providence. This year Paul took me to the house where the visionary writer passed the last decade of his too-brief life. Should you be interested, as of July 14, there was a "Studio for rent" sign outside the front door. I can already see the kernel for a short story — M. Dirda moves in, but soon grows increasingly reclusive, explaining that he's busy with researches into the suppressed Ur-text of *The Necronomicon* of the "mad Arab" Abdul Alhazred. When concerned friends finally knock at the door they discover the apartment inhabited by a gaunt, long-faced figure in old-fashioned black clothes. He explains that he is "subletting" from Mr. Dirda who was suddenly "called away." The air in the room is stale, with a peculiar fetor. . . .

Hmmm. Too obvious.

But what is Readercon, you ask? Readercon provides a chance for writers, editors, critics, and scholars to gather together and discuss science fiction. There are no masqueraders, no media tie-ins, no Hollywood celebrities — look for these at Comic-Con. This is a highly literary convention, built around four- to six-person panels, a dealer's room packed with new and used books, and a large hotel bar where people talk and drink late into the night.

When I say this is a serious conference, I mean it. Panels this year included: "Theological Debate in Fantasy and SF," "The Works of Shirley Jackson," "Genre Magazines in the 21st Century," "The Future of Copyright," "Book Covers Gone Wrong," the "Speculative Poetry Workshop," and perhaps 30 or 40 others. Peter Straub and Caitlin R. Kiernan were the two guests of honor. Regular attendees, besides those already mentioned, make up a who's who of fantastika's most honored writers and professionals — John Crowley, Samuel R. Delany, Ellen Datlow, David Hartwell, Michael Swanwick, Paul Park, Liza Groen Trombi, James and Kathryn Morrow, Joe and Gay Haldeman, Gregory Feeley, John Kessel, Kit Reed, Darrell Schweitzer, Jeff and Ann VanderMeer, Kathleen Ann Goonan, John Clute, Elizabeth Hand, Gordon Van Gelder, Graham Sleight, Kelly Link, and, a special treat this year, the doyenne of sf, Katherine Maclean. There are many others as well: This July, for instance, I ran into Bradford Morrow, editor of the literary magazine *Conjunctions.* Sometimes Junot Diaz comes, joking that he's just Chip Delany's driver. Alas, one pillar of the con, the brilliant, crotchety, and much-loved Barry Malzberg, was laid up in New Jersey this summer with severe knee and back ailments.

Every year I look forward to talking with most of these people, nearly all of whom I count as friends. But 2012 was different. Not only was I particularly busy with panels, but I also participated in a podcast, moderated by Karen Burnham, for Locus Magazine. For an hour and a half Locus's senior critic Gary K. Wolfe and I talked about reviewing, the state of the field, the breakdown of genre barriers, and the forthcoming *American Science Fiction: Nine Classic Novels of the 1950s.* This two-volume Library of America set, which Gary edited, doesn't publish until September, but you can already read essays about the chosen novels by William Gibson (on Alfred Bester's *The Stars My Destination*), Neil Gaiman (on Fritz Leiber's *The Big Time*), Connie Willis (on Robert A. Heinlein's *Double Star*), and others at the website www.loa.org/sciencefiction. The aforementioned M. Dirda writes about Cyril Kornbluth and Frederik Pohl's *The Space Merchants.*

This Readercon was different, too, in that I spent much of my time talking about old books, rather than new ones, with Robert Eldridge, Henry Wessells, and Robert Knowlton. All of them are professionally involved with the antiquarian book trade. Eldridge has been a cataloguer for the premier purveyor of collectible science fiction, L. W. Currey; Wessells works for the New York dealer James Cummins; and Knowlton is the manager for Contact Books in Toronto. The two Bobs also possess fabulous personal collections of rare fantasy, horror and sf — and seem to have read everything and remembered it all.

To spend time with these three isn't just a treat, it's an education. We chatted about such half-forgotten authors as Leonard Cline, Gerald Biss, Ann Bridge, Guy Boothby, Mervyn Wall, Frank Richardson and Kenneth Morris, discussed truly scarce novels such as *Swept & Garnished* by Donald Armour (a chilling work in need of a modern edition: see Eldridge's enthralling essay in the Autumn 2011 issue of the journal *Wormwood*), discovered our common enthusiasm for Peter Washington's *Madame Blavatsky's Baboon* (a history of Theosophy), and recalled unexpected treasures found in unexpected places. There is no better conversation in the world than talking about books with longtime dealers and collectors.

But then this is the joy of a science fiction and fantasy convention. Writers and readers mingle, you can say hello to a favorite author and get his or her books signed, there are tables piled high with paperbacks, fanzines, and old pulps such as *Thrilling Wonder Stories,* and you might even pick up a tee-shirt for your youngest son emblazoned "Bow Down Before Your Robot Masters" or a belt buckle depicting H. P. Lovecraft's dread Cthulhu. There are panels during the day and parties at night, and you are surrounded by people who share your own passions. Can life get any better?

Anyway, Readercon is over for this year, though I'm still recovering from its late nights and from downing more beer than I usually consume in a month. Happily, there's the regional Washington, D.C., convention Capclave to look forward to in October and then, in early November, the World Fantasy Convention in Toronto. Not even Cthulhu could keep me from being at this last: Bob Knowlton has promised to show me his library.

Aurora

Last Thursday evening my wife and I drove to Ohio, where we both grew up. Not having been "home" for several months, we'd begun to feel the usual guilt that plagues members of a family who move "out of state." No matter that we'd made that move more than 30 years ago.

En route, we listened to radio dramatizations of the adventures of Max Carrados, the blind detective invented by Ernest Bramah. (Bramah is almost as well known for his tall tales of Kai Lung, much prized for an artificial mock-Chinese style of the most punctilious politeness and irony.) The performances, starring Simon Callow, were excellent. At the end of each short mystery, an urbane announcer informed us that we had been enjoying "A Mr. Punch Production." Since the only person I know with a particular fondness for the name "Mr. Punch" is my multi-talented friend Neil

Gaiman, I wondered if this was one of his recent ventures. I do know Neil is a fan of Bramah's contemporaries, Arthur Conan Doyle and G. K. Chesterton, so this seemed more than likely. I figured I'd drop him a line the next day and just ask.

On Friday morning I said goodbye to my wife in Youngstown, where she would be helping her sister clean out their childhood home before putting it on the market, then drove to Lorain to visit my mother, who must now reside in an assisted living facility. I listened to music on the way — Arturo Benedetti Michelangeli's exhilarating performances of the Ravel G Major Piano Concerto and the Rachmaninoff No. 4 in G Minor. Since this Ohio trip was a last-minute idea, my mother practically choked on a mouthful of chicken sandwich when I unexpectedly appeared at her door. As I sat down to talk to her, she insisted that I phone my sisters Sandra, Pamela, and Linda to tell them I was in town. Only the last answered her phone, and the first thing Linda said was something about terrible killings in Colorado and was that anywhere near where my son Chris lived.

As it happened, the Aurora movie theater is about a 15 minutes' drive from my son's apartment in Denver.

I called him. No answer. I left a message asking him to communicate as soon as possible. I called my wife. No answer, so I left her a message asking her to try to reach Chris. I then called Chris's two brothers, neither of whom ever answers his phone when they see it's only their father, and left still more messages. By this time, my mother was starting to tremble with fright and worry. She wasn't quite keening, but she was close to it. While I tried to stay rational — he's got summer school classes, why would he go to the movies in the middle of the week? — my fears and imagination began, inexorably, to kick in. I almost never text on my ancient cell phone but I laboriously managed to spell out "CALLASAP." I never did figure out how to make word breaks.

An hour later Chris texted me back that he was in class and couldn't call and that he hadn't gone to the movies the night before. I was relieved. His mother, with her usual sang-froid, had figured he was okay all along. His grandmother, however, broke down in tears, and it took a while before she recovered her composure. I reprimanded Chris for not letting us know he was safe sooner.

But for an hour or two I experienced just

a tiny fraction of the nightmare that so many families and friends went through that Friday morning, as they waited to find out about their loved ones. Throughout my own anxiety I kept saying to myself, "He's sure to be okay," but I kept envisioning a friend stopping Chris after class and saying, "Hey, dude, a bunch of us are going to the midnight showing of the new Batman movie. Want to come?" On an impulse, Chris just might have gone along. As it happened, there was no invitation, and even if he had decided to catch the film he would probably have headed to a different theater. But it so easily could have been otherwise.

In that "otherwise" lies so much of the agony of the bereaved. Why? What if? Those impossible questions can never be answered, and yet they tear at our hearts. I don't presume to comprehend the grief, the unbearable grief, of those who lost friends and children in Aurora, or those who will live with the memory and wounds, physical and emotional, of that night. My mother is 89, and she will die one of these days, and I will be heartbroken. Yet this is the natural, the expected order of things: the old die, parents die. But not the young, not one's teenaged children, not like this.

In an editorial the other day my *Washing-*

ton Post colleague E. J. Dionne called wearily for reform to our gun laws. Such pleas have been going on for decades now. But somehow the National Rifle Association's lobbyists and supporters manage to override all common sense. It's an outrage. Semi-automatic weapons sold to 24-year-olds? Bullets bought freely over the Internet? Come on. We're not talking single-action .22s or Red Ryder BB guns. These days almost anyone can readily acquire what are, in essence, weapons of mass destruction.

There's an old story by the science fiction writer Fredric Brown. A stranger — possibly a visitor from the future — tries to persuade a scientist, on the brink of inventing the atom bomb or some similar doomsday weapon, to give up his research. The scientist argues that his work is pure; he is pursuing knowledge for its own ends. As it happens, this great genius has a beloved, but mentally handicapped child, who is playing in the next room. After the visitor leaves, unsuccessful in his mission, the father looks in on his son, who is fingering a new toy. Appalled, the scientist thinks: "Only a madman would give a loaded revolver to an idiot." Today, alas, we could say with even greater truth: "Only an idiot would give a loaded revolver to a madman."

Enough. We all mourn for those whose lives were ended or shattered in Aurora, at Virginia Tech, at Columbine — and who knows where next. But it will happen again. Unless guns are more closely regulated in this country, and anything more destructive than a hunting rifle restricted to the police or the armed forces, sooner or later we will all read the same horrible headlines once more. Only the faces will differ, only the death counts will be new.

[Note: On December 14, 2012, only a few months after I wrote the above, twenty very young children and six adults were shot to death in Newtown, Connecticut at Sandy Hook Elementary School.]

Out of Print

As readers grow older, their tastes often become more rarefied, more refined, more *recherché.* Certainly mine have. These days I gravitate increasingly to books almost no one else has heard of, let alone is interested in, books that are odd and quirky and usually out of print.

Simultaneously, I've also come to feel that if I don't write about a book in a review or essay, then I haven't actually read it. Gathering my thoughts, outlining an author's argument, framing a few apt quotations, trying to make inchoate impressions coherent — all these activities give substance to my experience of a work, make it real in a way that "reading" alone doesn't.

So given 1) this liking for the obscure and 2) my desire to write about what I've read, you may 3) glimpse my problem. Most literary publications don't publish essays, no matter how enthusiastic, about fiction or nonfiction that is out of print or otherwise unavailable. But suppose you want, as I do, to write about T. S. Stribling's satirical fantasy *These Bars of Flesh,* or Cutcliffe Hyne's Atlantis novel *The Lost Continent,* or Stella Benson's *Living Alone,* or Leonard Merrick's *The Man Who Understood Women,* or J. A. Mitchell's *Life's Fairy Tales,* or Amanda Ros's famously godawful *Irene Iddlesleigh* or any number of other worthwhile books that have fallen off our 21st-century radar. What can you do?

Usually, I just wait and hope that a small press or paperback house will reprint a book that interests me. For instance, by labeling them reviews, I could rhapsodize recently about William Lindsay Gresham's *Nightmare Alley,* J. R. Ackerley's *Hindoo Holiday,* and G. B. Edwards's *The Book of Ebenezer Le-Page* — all these reissued in handsome paperbacks from New York Review Books. Occasionally, too, some wise editor will ask me to reintroduce a lost classic. Because of a Barnes and Noble line of "rediscoveries," I was able to write short appreciations of Stendhal's *Memoirs of Egotism,* George Santayana's *Three Philosophical Poets,* and Anthony Burgess's *ABBA ABBA.* Specialized publishers by their very nature often seek out the lost and neglected. Tartarus Press generously invited me to contribute a foreword to *Tales of Love and Death,* a volume of Robert Aickman's wonderfully "strange" stories. A few years back, Night Shade Press requested introductions to the fantasies of Clark Ashton Smith and to Lord Dunsany's tall tales about Joseph Jorkens. Barbara and Christopher Roden solicited a preface to an Ash-Tree Press collection of Arthur Conan Doyle's short supernatural fiction. I remain immensely grateful for these opportunities.

But will the chance ever come to write about Vincent McHugh's fantasy *I Am Thinking of My Darling* (in which people lose all moral constraints) or William Plomer's *The Diamond of Jannina: Ali Pasha, 1741– 1822* (once praised for its author's prose style by Edmund White), or the four Great Merlini mysteries of Clayton Rawson (who grew up in Elyria, Ohio, eight miles from my hometown of Lorain), or the historical swashbucklers of Stanley Weyman, or *G.B.,* by W. F. Morris, once selected by Eric Ambler as one of the five best spy novels of all time? Who knows?

As you can guess, I own all these books. They have been patiently gathered over the years, though I have often been guided by knowledgeable friends. For instance, Mark

Valentine, editor of the journal *Wormwood: Writings About Fantastic, Supernatural and Decadent Literature,* recommended *G.B.* (also known as *Bretherton*). Bob Eldridge, whom I mentioned in the recent column about Readercon, suggested that I look into the work of Clemence Dane, Gerald Bullett and Martin Armstrong. He himself introduced a welcome reissue of Emma Dawson's supernatural fiction *An Itinerant House.* Tolkien scholar Douglas Anderson, who runs a blog called "Lesser Known Writers," urged me to try David Lindsay's gigantic fantasy *Devil's Tor,* currently available only through a print-on-demand publisher. Of course, most book sections don't review POD publications. While I've written about Lindsay's famous *A Voyage to Arcturus,* will I ever find a venue in which to explore *Devil's Tor?* Or Maurice Baring's *Daphne Adeane* or the novels of Claude Farrère or T. F. Powys's *Mr. Weston's Good Wine* or Elinor Wylie's *The Venetian Glass Nephew?*

There is one possibility. . . .

Let this be fair warning: It may come about that I will, from time to time, interrupt the usual personalia and literary musings of "Browsings" to present, instead, a little essay about some odd or forgotten volume that has caught my attention and deserves yours. I hope you won't mind such occasional pieces. Indeed, I hope you'll enjoy them.

[Note: I never really followed through on this threat or promise. But I have written, and continue to write, about neglected books quite frequently and hope, some day, to collect some of these essays. Others may be repurposed for my current project, a study of popular fiction during the late 19th and early 20th centuries.]

THRIFT STORIES

Last Saturday morning I visited Antiques Row in Kensington, Maryland, my mission being to accompany my wife to the farmers' market there. But as my Beloved Spouse began to check out the organic produce and baked goods, I naturally enough wandered away to the Prevention of Blindness thrift store across the street. I believe I whistled as I did so, and my step was jaunty.

I am something of an aficionado of thrift stores. In my youth, I regularly searched their shelves for old books. In fact, Clarice's Values in my hometown of Lorain, Ohio, supplied a sizable portion of my early reading matter. There I bought science fiction and mystery paperbacks for a nickel apiece and sometimes unearthed finds such as the second American printing of *Ulysses*. A price of 45 cents was scribbled on its front endpaper with a crayon, but I may have talked Clarice down from that. Once, in a fit of utter madness, I purchased a complete set of the novels of Sir Walter Scott for $5. Getting them home — I was a 15-year-old on a bicycle — was, shall we say, challenging.

Here in D.C., the major secondhand emporiums — Goodwill, Value Village, and their ilk — only seem to stock fairly recent best-sellers, cookbooks, and the complete works of James Patterson. In short, the sort of titles they feel are "salable." I, by contrast, am mainly interested in books published before I was born, largely by authors who are now virtually forgotten. What I like to see on bookcases or steel shelves are lots of pre-World War II fiction, most of it looking just slightly better than shabby.

Despite my rather eclectic taste, one fateful day, at the Georgia Avenue Thrift Shop, I couldn't find a single book of interest and so decided to look around the rest of the store. For some reason I meandered down a row of men's shirts, just fingering them idly until I noticed a half dozen dressy ones in a row. They were obviously by the same maker and two were white, two were cream, and two were blue. I soon observed three further salient details: 1) the shirts had French cuffs; 2) the initials LES were stitched just above the holes for the left-sleeve cufflink;

and 3) they had been made in France by a company called Charvet.

I knew nothing then about men's fashion or tailoring, but I could tell that these elegant garments were a cut above your ordinary J.C. Penney's wash-and-wear. They were also my size — 15 1/2 neck, 33-inch sleeve — and each was marked $2. Since I bought all six the cashier let me have the lot for 10 bucks. Through the wonders of my computer search engine — this was before Google was ubiquitous — I learned that my new acquisitions were quite exceptionally good shirts. Expensive shirts. In fact, the kind of shirts that Gatsby would keep in his closet to impress Daisy Buchanan. As a result, on those rare occasions when I'm invited to a classy dinner or semiformal event, I tend to wear one of these Charvets. People sometimes ask about the monogram LES on my cuff, since they're obviously not my initials. Putting on a conspiratorial air, I quietly hint that Michael Dirda is just one of many names I use and that there's far more to my life than just sitting at a keyboard writing book reviews and columns for *The American Scholar.* If only.

But every blessing, it's been said, is also a curse, and today I'm not entirely sure that my discovery of those designer shirts was an entirely good piece of luck. Mine is not a temperate nature. A little too much is just enough for me.

I soon started to read *GQ* and *Esquire,* acquired copies of the complete works of Alan Flusser, the leading authority on men's clothes, studied websites like Will Boehlke's "A Suitable Wardrobe" (very upmarket) and Giuseppe Timore's exceptionally lively "An Affordable Wardrobe." At the same time I took to stopping by thrift stores everywhere, seeking other ritzy garments at bargain prices. I now own enough shirts from Thomas Pink, Burberry, and Brooks Brothers to outfit a Wall Street brokerage house or major law firm. My attic is packed tight with suits by Armani, Brioni, and Canali, as well as the rest of the alphabet, all the way down to Zegna. There are vintage J. Press jackets, cashmere sweaters galore, and a collection of shoes that the late Imelda Marcos would have envied — though none of mine boast stiletto heels.

Had I begun this "hobby" 20 years ago, I might be able to justify or at least rationalize this sartorial excess. But do I now go to an office every day? No. Do I attend lots of fancy parties and receptions? No. Do I work as a banker or professional escort to women of a certain age? No. Do I really need more than three or four good suits and the same number of sport jackets? No.

This past spring I loved teaching at the University of Maryland in part because I could dress up for class. I didn't repeat an outfit the entire semester. The only other time I tend to wear a jacket and tie — did I mention my tie and pocket square collection? — is when I give a talk. And even then I often feel overdressed. Authors these days are expected to wear jeans, work shirts, and a ratty blue blazer.

Having three sons — now all in their 20s — I've been able to pass along some of my thrift shop treasures. But my strapping offspring are taller and skinnier than I am, so a lot of my "pieces" don't work for them. But I'm happy knowing that if they need to be dressed up, they own the clothes to do it with.

Friends tell me that I should sell the designer suits and Sulka ties on eBay. That sounds like a lot of work — taking pictures, figuring out measurements, packing and shipping, keeping records. Once I did try a consignment shop, which took some of the better jackets and suits, sold half of them, and never paid me a penny. The check was always in the mail.

No, I suppose that what I'll do is reseed

the thrift stores of greater Washington. One of these days some idealistic young bookworm will be browsing through Value Village, on the lookout for a first edition of *The Great Gatsby,* and instead he'll come across some Charvet shirts. . . . There won't be six of them, though. I'm keeping at least two, maybe three, just in case I'm asked to the White House for a long weekend.

MUSICAL CHAIRS

Last week I mentioned a visit to the Prevention of Blindness thrift shop in Kensington, Maryland. Doesn't ring a bell, you say? Well, let's just note that attentive students of this column, men and women of intelligence, refinement, and exceptional good looks, will recall that I had escaped from the local farmers' market to seek out more substantial treasures than whole wheat bread and organic squash, just the kind of treasures, in fact, that St. Matthew warns us against storing up on this earth and that are prey to moth and rust.

Somehow this led to a column about Charvet shirts and thrift stores.

As it happens, I didn't buy any clothes at the Prevention of Blindness shop — oh, okay, I couldn't resist a green Richel tie with ducks on it — but I did pick up a dozen compact discs. Each was a dollar, and many were obviously the former property of a Maria Callas fan. But why had he — Callas fans tend to be he — divested himself of the diva's repertory? Was he (or possibly she) now worshipping at the feet of Renée Fleming or Angela Gheorghiu? There was *Maria Callas: Live in Milan 1956 and Athens 1957,* as well as several operas: *Madama Butterfly, Lucia di Lammermoor, Carmen.*

While I left a good many other CDs that I already owned, I still brought home Scarlatti's *Stabat Mater* (with The Sixteen, under Harry Christophers), Leonard Bernstein conducting *Favorite Russian Spectaculars,* Puccini's *Turandot* with Birgit Nilsson, Renata Tebaldi and Jussi Björling (my favorite tenor), an album of Elizabethan songs called *Shakespeare's Kingdom,* featuring mezzo-soprano Sarah Walker and pianist Graham Johnson, Stravinsky's *Apollon Musagète,* performed by the Scottish Chamber Orchestra under Jukka-Pekka Saraste, and Michael Tilson Thomas conducting Gershwin's *Of Thee I Sing* and *Let 'em Eat Cake.*

Good music, all of it, and cheap. Which is the disturbing part. Compact discs are clearly on the way out.

It wasn't so long ago — 25 or 30 years — that CDs first appeared and began to oust vinyl records and audio cassettes as the preferred medium for serious music. For me, this development was a real boon. In my younger days I used to visit record shops and covet boxed sets of Beethoven symphonies, Wagner operas, Bach cantatas, Mozart piano concertos. Only rarely was I able to find the money for such luxuries. I do know that the first opera I ever owned — I still have it — was Mozart's *Don Giovanni,* the classic performance with a star-studded cast under the baton of Carlo Maria Giulini.

But once CDs, supposedly unscratchable and permanent, entered the market, collectors began to dump their vinyl. You could buy an opera for a few dollars, readily pick up multiple versions of Berlioz's *Symphonie Fantastique* or the Brahms violin concerto, find spoken-arts rarities like Charles Laughton reading stories from the Bible — no one ever forgets his performance of Shadrach, Meshach and Abednego in "the burning fiery furnace" — or even acquire the original Broadway cast performance of *Waiting for Godot.* As my old car's sound system only played cassettes, I also snatched up lots of cassettes, usually for a quarter apiece. I found taped lectures from The Teaching Company deaccessioned at the local library, heart-breaker collections of Patsy Cline, Lorrie Morgan, and Reba McEntire, the unabridged *Lolita* read by Jeremy Irons.

As a result, my LPs soon overflowed their shelves, and the cassettes filled up entire plastic bins. Worse still, I gradually began to be lured into acquiring compact discs. Used bookshops sometimes stocked secondhand CDs, and I started to trade glossy hardbacks for irresistible boxed sets of Ella Fitzgerald singing the American Songbook and Mitsuko Uchida playing the Mozart piano sonatas. When the CDs needed more space, more and more of the vinyl and tape migrated into the basement.

And then one day my kids began to download music from the Internet. Before long they wanted iPods and iPod docks as Christmas gifts. As usual, I didn't notice the writing on the wall and blithely went on buying cheap records, tapes, and CDs. Champagne culture on a beer budget — what could be better?

Still, when music that once cost 20 dollars a disc is selling for a buck, you shouldn't need an angelic hand to write "Mene, Mene, Tekel Upharsin" to realize that the days of the CD are numbered.

Which they obviously are. But I'm not sure I'll be making the switch to downloaded music (or downloaded books, for that matter). My much-missed *Book World* colleague Reid Beddow used to say, "The old ways are best," and part of me certainly believes this about records. If you bought Cimarosa's *Il Matrimonio Segreto* or Benjamin Britten's *Peter Grimes,* it once came in a substantial box, with a full libretto in multiple languages. Sometimes there was even a score, as well as a booklet with an essay on the opera and its composer, pictures of the performers and conductor, brief biographies and discographies of everyone involved. The cover of the boxed set might reproduce a painting, perhaps something by Fragonard or Watteau. Every aspect of this lavishness announced that this was an important work of music, deserving one's care, attention, love, and money.

No more. Audiotape and compact discs started to reduce this extra-musical *richesse.* And now we're down to the bare bones: You simply press a button on your MP3 player and the music begins. It's easy, it's convenient. You want more information — look online. But hasn't just a bit of the magic, something of the beauty and aura of the performance disappeared? I think so.

Where your treasure is, there will your heart be also. Even now I keep a few vinyl albums in frames, and not just for the gorgeous covers, though, I must admit, one features a portrait of Elisabeth Schwarzkopf looking more glamorous than Greta Garbo, and another, of Erich Korngold's music for *The Sea Hawk,* shows two great sailing ships closing for combat. Most of all, though, I still play the records and CDs in my collection, and sometimes even my audio tapes. The old ways may not always be best, but they still work for me.

THE EVIDENCE
IN THE (BOOK) CASE

Readers of crime novels know that much can be determined about victims or suspected murderers by taking notice of the titles on their bookshelves. A copy of the *Handbook of Chemistry and Physics* with underlinings on the page devoted to toxic alkalis may generally be construed as a dead giveaway. Bound volumes of *Soldier of Fortune* magazine might similarly hint that there might be more to the victim — supposedly a pacifist vegetarian Buddhist — than just yogic meditation.

You can tell a lot about a writer, too, from the books stacked on his or her nightstand, or strewn on the floor next to the bed. Or can you? To test this theory, I'm going to list — in no particular order — some of the bookish items I keep close to my pillow for late-night browsing. Most of these fall loosely under the category of reference works and anthologies.

Wodehouse Nuggets, selected by Richard Usborne. Quotations from the Master: "As he reached the end of the carpet and was about to turn about and pace back again, he stopped abruptly with one foot in the air looking so much like *The Soul's Awakening* that a seasoned art critic would have been deceived."

ABC for Book Collectors (Fifth edition), by John Carter. More a series of witty mini-essays than just a lexicon of bibliographical terms. "Sophisticated: This adjective, as applied to a book, is simply a polite synonym for doctored or faked-up."

The Guide to Supernatural Fiction, by E. F. Bleiler. An expert on Victorian and early 20th-century science fiction, fantasy, and horror, Bleiler offers capsule summaries and brief judgments on hundreds of novels and tales of the supernatural. Of E. R. Eddison's *The Worm Ouroboros,* he succinctly concludes: "Still the finest heroic fantasy." One of the great works of one-man scholarship.

The Faber Popular Reciter, selected by Kingsley Amis; *Famous Poems from Bygone Days* and *Best Remembered Poems,* both edited by Martin Gardner. Three volumes of the kind of old-fashioned poetry that people used to declaim in church halls and under the Chautauqua tents: "Backward, turn backward, O Time, in your flight,/ Make me a child again just for tonight!" (Elizabeth Akers Allen)

The Tough Guide to Fantasyland, by Diana Wynne Jones. A dictionary of the *"idées reçues"* of fantasy fiction, set down by one of the genre's finest authors: "**Alleys** are the most frequent type of **Road** in a **City** or **Town.** They are always narrow and dark and squishy, and they frequently dead-end. You will escape along them when pursued and also be **Ambushed** there."

The Pléiade edition of Voltaire's *Romans et Contes.* As Somerset Maugham once said, if you would write perfectly, you would write like Voltaire.

Quotable Sherlock, compiled by David W. Barber: "You have degraded what should have been a course of lectures into a series of tales." *Quotable Alice,* compiled by David W. Barber: " 'And what is the use of a book,' thought Alice, 'without pictures or conversations?' "

A Catalogue of Crime, by Jacques Barzun and Wendell Hertig Taylor. An annotated listing of detective fiction and true-crime nonfiction. Idiosyncratic and provocative — the authors favor the classic puzzle rather than modern ultra-violence — but no less magisterial for that. One favorite recommendation: *The Murder of Sir Edmund Godfrey,* a "true-crime" masterpiece by that specialist in the locked-room puzzle, John Dickson Carr.

Edward Gorey's *The Unstrung Harp* and *The Curious Sofa: A Pornographic Work by Ogdred Weary:* "Alice, quite exhausted, was helped to bed by Lady Celia's French maid, Lise, whom she found delightfully sympathetic."

Three omnibus volumes of *Christmas Crackers:* Quotations from the commonplace book of John Julius Norwich. I love commonplace books; the most recent entry in my own is from the photographer Alfred Stieglitz: "Nearly right is child's play."

Collected Books: The Guide to Identification and Values, by Allen and Patricia Ahearn (fourth edition); *Guide to First Edition Prices,* by R. B. Russell (8th edition). Whenever I browse in these pages and see what some modern firsts are going for, I realize I should take better care of my books.

The Hundred Headless Women and *Une Semaine de Bonté,* both by Max Ernst. Two exceptionally disturbing graphic novels by the great surrealist. Similar collagist masterpieces: E. V. Lucas and George Morrow's lighthearted *What A Life!* and Tom Phillips's touching *A Humument: A Treated Victorian Novel* (four editions, all different, all necessary).

An inscribed album of Gahan Wilson's macabre cartoons. My favorite: several seedy, unshaven guys, sporting crooked haloes and dressed in dingy robes, are standing near a broken lopsided sign that reads, "Heaven." One guy, clearly dismayed, says to his neighbor: "Somehow, I thought the whole thing would be a lot classier."

Life Is Meals: A Food Lover's Book of Days, by James and Kay Salter, who are two of my favorite people (and he is one of our finest writers). Each day brings its own short essay: January 3 is "Dinner with Lord Byron"; March 24, "Waiters"; May 23, "Michelin Guide"; December 22, "Candy Canes."

Geary's Guide to the World's Great Aphorists, compiled by James Geary. "In skating over thin ice our safety is in our speed." — Emerson; "God will forgive me. It's his job." — Heine.

The Gramophone Classical Music Guide (several editions). Should I try Simone Dinnerstein or Angela Hewitt in Bach's *Goldberg Variations?* Or shall I just stick with Glenn Gould's exceedingly slow, and immensely moving, 1981 recording?

The Englishman's Room, edited by Alvilde Lees-Milne. Pictures — by Derry Moore — of libraries, studies and book-strewn living rooms, each accompanied by an essay: The stuff of Anglophile daydreams.

The Encyclopedia of Science Fiction, edited by John Clute and Peter Nicholls, et al.; *The Encyclopedia of Fantasy,* edited by John Clute, John Grant, et al. The most intelligent literary reference books in the world.

The Literary Life: A Scrapbook Almanac of the Anglo-American Literary Scene from 1900 to 1950, by Robert Phelps and Peter Deane. Its principal author, Robert Phelps, was the first "literary man" I ever met — and the kindest and best.

The Essays, Articles and Reviews of Evelyn Waugh. Our anti-modern Voltaire.

Despite all these books being close at hand, I still tend to gravitate to specialized periodicals at bedtime. Some of my favorites include *All Hallows: The Journal of the Ghost Story Society; Wormwood: Literature of the Fantastic, Supernatural and Decadent; Locus,* the trade magazine of science fiction and fantasy; *The Baker Street Journal; Extraordinary Voyages: The Newsletter of the North American Jules Verne Society; Knight Letter,* the magazine of the Lewis Carroll Society of North America; old issues of *Million: The Magazine About Popular Fiction;* and *The Journal of the Arthur Conan Doyle Society.*

Like many other people, I also find several Asian classics particularly restful late at night, especially the works of Chuang Tzu, Mencius, and Confucius. The *Tao Te Ching,* in particular, offers not only gnomic injunctions on how to live but at least one essential piece of advice for any writer: "Know when to stop."

CHARLOTTESVILLE

A few weeks back I received, from out of the blue, an email from the Association for Documentary Editing (ADE). This isn't, I should point out, a professional organization for cinematographers who specialize in the kind of movies shown at the Silverdocs festival of the American Film Institute. In fact, the ADE represents those learned folk who oversee great scholarly editions of, for instance, the papers of George Washington, the works of Ralph Waldo Emerson, the archives of Willa Cather.

Why were they emailing me?

It turns out that every two years the ADE awards the Boydston Prize for the best review or essay, "the primary focus of which is the editing of a volume of works or documents." This year's winner turned out to be — well, aw shucks — me. The award committee was quite taken with a long essay-review I'd written for *The New York Review of Books* comparing two annotated editions of *The Wind in the Willows.*

Need I say that I was incredibly chuffed (to use a British verb I'm fond of)? As Harriet Simon, editor of the John Dewey papers, generously said, the piece I wrote "gives the strengths of each edition but also points out such pitfalls as misreadings, misprinted citations, oversights, and bemoans the lack of critical attention to the book's inner structure, especially its leitmotifs and verbal repetitions."

When asked if I would come to the ADE's annual convention to receive the award at the Friday night banquet, I immediately agreed. Happily, this only meant a two-and-a-half-hour drive to one of my favorite cities, Charlottesville, Virginia.

I arrived there at 2 P.M. on a Thursday, checked into a Budget Inn, and immediately set off for the city's downtown pedestrian mall. Lined with shops and restaurants, packed with tourists searching for souvenirs and local teens just hanging out, it's one of Cville's main attractions. It is also the location for three used-bookstores, with two others not far away. All the shops are worth checking out, and two are especially strong in older science fiction and mysteries, but I beelined for the biggest, just off the mall on

4th St: Daedalus Books.

Three hours later I emerged, without buying anything.

To my surprise, the store closed at five, long before I had completed my systematic inspection of its labyrinthine fiction-rich basement. So I simply deposited a box of my selections at the front desk and promised to return the next morning. As I left, I asked if any of the other bookshops might still be open? Yes. Read It Again Sam didn't close till eight.

So I passed another couple of hours there, and bought three books: *The Other Passenger,* by John Keir Cross, a 1946 collection of fantasy stories in a near-fine dust jacket; a Folio Society volume entitled *Lord Byron and Some of His Contemporaries,* compiled by Joanna Richardson; and *Nightmare: The Birth of Horror,* by Christopher Frayling. This last, based on four BBC television programs, is a lovely picture book, with excellent chapters on *Frankenstein, Dracula, The Strange Case of Dr Jekyll and Mr Hyde,* and *The Hound of the Baskervilles.* Years ago I reviewed Frayling's terrific biography of filmmaker Sergio Leone, then later invited him to address the Sherlockians of The Baker Street Irregulars, which eventually made him a member.

That evening I got back to my motel around 8:30, quickly washed the book dust from my face, and then hurried across the street to an Italian eatery, where I devoured nearly all of a small deluxe pizza. Along with a cold beer. Why not? It had been a very good day.

Friday was even better. That morning I stopped at the Virginia Book Company, which was going out of business, and found on its half-emptied shelves a beautiful copy of *A Desert Drama,* the American title given to Arthur Conan Doyle's *The Tragedy of the 'Korosko.'* In this eerily contemporary novel, Middle Eastern terrorists kidnap a group of western tourists, intending to sell the younger women, including a recent American college graduate, into slavery and execute the men — unless they all convert to Islam. Will they? Can they? Sir Arthur works the suspense and the melodrama for all they're worth.

Once I got back to Daedalus I bought the previous day's books, along with a few more items unearthed that morning. One was a copy of a school novel called *Decent Fellows,* by an old Etonian named John Heygate, now remembered, if at all, for being the co-respondent in the shattering breakup of Evelyn Waugh's first marriage. (Waugh said: "I did not know it was possible to be so miserable and live.") Then it was off to Heartwood, a used-book store located near the University of Virginia campus. I bought more books there — including a so-so first American edition of H. G. Wells's *In the Days of the Comet,* which I later realized I already owned (albeit in an even more dilapidated condition). By this time, though, I found myself feeling increasingly guilty, seeing that it was the middle of the afternoon and I was really supposed to be at the Omni to listen in on some of the ADE panels.

I sauntered into the hotel's lobby with perfect timing: one panel had just let out, people were standing around chatting over coffee and cake, and I was soon saying hello to Harriet Simon, who quickly introduced me to a half dozen of her colleagues. I caught the last panel of the afternoon — focusing on a governmental report on the needs of scholarly editors — and then had time to freshen up before the cocktail party and banquet.

At dinner I found myself seated with the officers of the ADE and several people who worked at either Monticello, the University of Virginia Press, or a special institute devoted to the Thomas Jefferson papers. Charlottesville is, of course, ever and always Mr. Jefferson's town. Over conversation I discovered that one of my tablemates collected 19th-century "Boy's Books," in particular those series featuring the adventurous Rover Boys, Gunboat Boys, and similar daring youths. I couldn't have asked for better company or conversation.

Halfway through the evening's ceremonies I was presented with my plaque, as well as a small honorarium. When the banquet was over, many of my new friends were off to enjoy a nightcap at the hotel bar. But, alas, I couldn't join them. My eldest son was arriving from Colorado that night, and the Dirda family was then leaving for two days at the beach. So, just as a violent thunderstorm hit, I drove out of Charlottesville, got lost, asked for directions, and gradually made my way to Washington, where the Beltway was backed up due to either an accident or construction, enough to convince a certain frustrated Boydston Prize-winner to drive off into mysterious northern Virginia at 1 A.M., get completely lost again, plaintively beg for directions at a 7-Eleven, and then finally grope his way back to Silver Spring, Maryland, center of civilization. If ever there was a driver who needed a GPS system, I am that driver.

On my little excursion, I obviously spent more money on books than I should have. 'Twas ever thus. But, hey, I was on "vacation," away from my family and surrounded by bookstores I didn't get to visit very often, so really, what else could I have done? Besides, my honorarium from the Boydston Prize almost exactly covered my book purchases. In fact, I came out ahead by a few dollars. Best of all, I'd met some fascinating people, learned a lot more about scholarly editing, and returned home with a standing invitation to a private tour of Monticello.

Then and Now

A few days ago I arrived back in Lorain, Ohio — where I grew up — to spend some time with my mother, who now resides in a nursing home. Her mind is still sharp and she plays a mean game of 500 Rummy, but the after-effects of a stroke have kept her wheelchair bound and rendered her right hand useless. Once upon a time I sat in my mother's lap, as she turned the pages of Golden Books and I gradually learned to read. These days I bring her children's picture books, which we enjoy looking at together before she puts them aside as gifts for her first great-grandchild.

Every day when I walk through the hallways of this "long-term care facility," I see rows of the aged, seated in their wheelchairs, with heads turtled down. Aside from weekly bingo, occasional ice cream socials, and makeshift church services, there's simply not a whole lot for them to do. In general, the residents watch television and live from meal to meal: People start rolling themselves into the dining room a little after 4, even though dinner isn't served until 5. Sometimes, in the evenings, I hear a screamer shrieking for help or find myself accosted by a pathetic weeping woman who wants me to take her home. One handsome if vacant-minded patient regularly raises an arm high above her wheelchair-throne to bestow a regal wave that Queen Elizabeth would envy. It's all quite heartbreaking.

When I come to visit my Mom — every two or three months — I generally spend five or six hours with her each day. She's always immensely glad to see me, her eldest child, her only son. My three younger sisters live in the area, and they stop by regularly, wash her clothes, bring her favorite foods. But it's hard on the whole family. My mother's savings are gone, she's now on Medicaid, and later this fall the government will try to sell her house. The real estate market in this derelict steel town is, needless to say, pretty dismal. On my mother's block alone several homes have been on the market for months, even years. Asking prices probably range around $40,000 or so. A house two doors away recently went for $25,000.

I do stay in my mother's house, my boyhood home, whenever I visit. In recent years the downstairs has been gradually taken over by dolls. There are dolls on the mantel, in glass cabinets, on shelves, on the floor. Many are of Shirley Temple; one — which might actually be worth something — is a two-foot-tall Princess Diana in her wedding dress. Other than my mother's dolls, the rest of the ground floor had been decorated, until recently, in Home Nursing Care. Accent items included boxes of adult diapers, catheters, trays of meds and skin creams, a hospital bed, a Hoyer lift, and a folding wheelchair.

As you might imagine, my emotions are complicated when I visit. Now that my mother isn't using my old ground-floor bedroom, I've taken to staying in it again. Half a century ago my father built this "addition," largely because the house only had two bedrooms upstairs and I was growing too old to share one of them with my sisters. My mother, in the way of mothers, eventually decorated this room — after I'd left — with pictures of me and framed newspaper articles about the honors that have come my way, mainly due to hard work and luck rather than any exceptional talent. Still, it's all a little embarrassing. My middle sister,

Pam, regularly razzes me about the "shrine."

These days, lying in bed, I can again look up at the wall shelves my father installed for my youthful book collection. Many of the original books are gone — they're in a basement in Silver Spring — but others are still here. In the mornings, waiting to find the energy to face another day, I sometimes scan the titles that remain: *Roy Rogers and Dale Evans in River of Peril, The Silken Baroness Contract, How to Make More Money, Essentials of Marxism, Litterature Comparée: L'Etude des Thèmes.* Throughout my adolescence, I would study in this room after supper, then read for hour after hour, until my mother, in her old nightgown, would pad down the stairs and say, "Mikey, it's 2 o'clock in the morning. Go to sleep."

In very rare, Gatsbyish moments I sometimes think, "Well, boy, you've come a long way." But most of the time, when I gaze upon my beloved mother in her wheelchair or stand at my father's grave, I just tend to grow thoughtful, which is a slightly more genteel way of saying depressed. I miss my young parents. I miss the boy I used to be. Leon Trotsky, no less, once said: "Old age is the most unexpected of all the things that happen to a man."

In fact, I even miss this down-at-heels

steeltown. Looking out from the McDonald's in which I'm writing, I can just make out the site of the old branch library, once an integral part of the Lorain Plaza Shopping Center. For years I'd ride my bike over every week or two, browse through the old-fashioned bookcases, then check out *The Mysterious Island* or *Atlas Shrugged* or *A Shropshire Lad.* Of course, that branch library is long gone, replaced first by a Radio Shack, then a cell-phone store. It's now a second-rate pizza joint, just waiting to become a Dollar General.

Sigh. Since adolescence one of my favorite poems has been Ernest Dowson's *"Non sum qualis eram bonae sub regno Cynarae."* This is the one with the famous line, "I have been faithful to thee, Cynara, in my fashion." Its Latin title can be roughly paraphrased and severely shortened to: "Things aren't as good as they used to be." Driving home after spending an evening with my mother, I wonder: Is there a room in a nursing home waiting for me? How many good years do I have left? . . . As my father used to say: "Live fast."

In fact, I've lived slow, dithered and dallied, taken my own sweet time, and done pretty much what I've repeatedly done ever since my mother first taught me to read so long ago: Found a quiet spot and opened a book. When I turned 50 I remember thinking that just maybe I should have spent fewer hours in libraries and more drunken nights in dives and honky-tonks. Maybe. Maybe not. I'll never know.

Still, just the other day I noticed *The Golden Argosy* on my old bookshelves. I discovered this anthology of stories at the age of 12 or 13 — it is, I recently learned, one of Stephen King's favorite books. Of its many great selections, my own rather tell-tale favorite was Joseph Conrad's "Youth." Half a century later, I can still remember when I first read its carefully cadenced, if syntactically challenging, final sentences, among the greatest dying falls of English literature:

" 'But you here — you all had something out of life: money, love — whatever one gets on shore — and, tell me, wasn't that the best time, that time when we were young at sea; young and had nothing, on the sea that gives nothing, except hard knocks — and sometimes a chance to feel your strength — that only — what you all regret?'

"And we all nodded at him: the man of finance, the man of accounts, the man of law, we all nodded at him over the polished table that like a still sheet of brown water

reflected our faces, lined, wrinkled; our
faces marked by toil, by deceptions, by success, by love; our weary eyes looking still,
looking always, looking anxiously for something out of life, that while it is expected is
already gone — has passed unseen, in a
sigh, in a flash — together with the youth,
with the strength, with the romance of illu-
sions."

MENCKEN DAY

Last Saturday my wife and I drove up to Baltimore for Mencken Day. This is the annual celebration, held at the Enoch Pratt Free Library, honoring Henry Louis Mencken (1880–1956), our country's most famous, or notorious, journalist, the self-appointed scourge of the philistines.

During the day's festivities, a morning session is devoted to a meeting of The Mencken Society, with a speaker, and the afternoon to the annual Mencken Memorial Lecture. Last year I pronounced the afternoon talk, my subject being "The Literary Journalist in the Age of H. L. Mencken." I focused mainly on the Chicago bookman Vincent Starrett, the *Saturday Review of Literature* columnist Christopher Morley, and, just in passing, that long-lived man of letters and Book-of-the-Month Club judge, Clifton Fadiman.

Last year, being flattered to have addressed the Mencken Society, I felt that the least I could do was join it. Just as rich people congregate at country clubs and crackpots form secret societies, I seem to gravitate to small and specialized literary groups to which I contribute annual dues and occasionally lend somewhat more active support. Some of these organizations, honoring Jules Verne, Lewis Carroll, Edgar Rice Burroughs, and Sherlock Holmes, were mentioned in an earlier column. Besides these, I once belonged to the Tilling Society, an association for admirers of E. F. Benson's comic Lucia novels, and plan to rejoin the Friends of Arthur Machen, devotees of the multi-talented author best known for his supernatural fiction, notably *The Great God Pan* and "The White People," the latter one of the genre's supreme masterpieces. I am also proud to be a member of much larger entities such as the Mystery Writers of America and the Science Fiction Writers of America.

It nonetheless surprises me that I've become involved, however minimally, with all these associations and sodalities. For most of my life, I've regarded myself as a non-joiner, suspicious of any sort of collective behavior or corporate *bonhomie*. It was a source of pride that my college, Oberlin, prohibited fraternities and sororities. Every sort of Rotarian glad-handing appalls me. Crowds tend to oppress my spirits. I identify with Kipling's "Cat that walked by himself."

And, yet, I've discovered, you have to get out, you do need to see other human beings. You can't just read and write all day, much as I'd like to. After a few hours in a chair, my body grows achy, my brain feels even mushier than usual, my tired eyes start to hurt. To refresh myself I usually go for a walk, or, if I'm feeling virtuous and resolute, I'll hike over to the gym to lift weights or run on the treadmill. At other times, I just change my workplace, often heading to the library — where I'm typing now — simply to be surrounded by other people while I read or write. It's somehow relaxing to hear patrons asking about recorded books, or glimpse high-school students quietly flirting.

Years ago, when I was in graduate school, I took to polishing chapters of my dissertation late at night in a local McDonald's. It should have been distracting, as truckers, prostitutes and police officers dropped by after midnight for coffee or Big Macs. It wasn't. I remember feeling astonishingly serene, with my three-ring binder of notes and the 300-page rough draft of my analysis of Stendhal's autobiographical *La Vie de Henry Brulard.*

Did I know then that Bertolt Brecht liked to write his plays in rooms filled with people, in effect, at parties? He felt it kept him connected with his audience. I was certainly aware that Sartre, Simone de Beauvoir, and all the other existentialists scribbled their treatises and novels and poems over cups of espresso at the Café de Flore or La Rotonde. The air here in the library is fresh, and the susurration of low voices surprisingly restful, a background hum like that produced by those white-noise sleep machines. Of course, I always feel happy in libraries and bookstores. They restoreth my soul.

My affiliation with literary sodalities provides a similar kind of R and R. I love the bookish shoptalk. Being around collectors and passionate readers, whether of *Alice's Adventures in Wonderland* or the Tarzan books or the *Voyages Extraordinaires,* is exhilarating. I get caught up in other people's enthusiasm for their favorite authors. Before I know it, I'm daydreaming about spending a winter reading all of Burroughs or Horatio Alger Jr., or of collecting the Hetzel editions of Jules Verne, or of writing a study of classic children's authors.

After the morning lecture, by H. George Hahn on Mencken's satire, Marian and I had a little time before lunch, so we visited the impressive Basilica of the Assumption across the street from the Pratt library: If the Shakers or Zen Buddhists were to design a Catholic cathedral, it might look like this — plain white walls and fixtures, an elegant dome, brilliant natural sunlight streaming in, a design of classical simplicity and clarity. After one awed glance, my wife immediately murmured that the church might almost be the work of Benjamin Latrobe, the architect of the Capitol. As it turned out, it was.

We stayed for the afternoon talk, in which Richard Schrader revealed how slanted and inaccurate Mencken's account of the Scopes evolution trial had been, and afterwards chatted a bit over cookies and punch with some members of the Mencken Society and a young guy who turned out to be chairman of the North American Discworld Convention. He reminded me that the con — a celebration of the fantasy fiction of Terry Pratchett — would be in Baltimore next year. I suspect I'll be there. [I was.] How can I resist becoming involved with yet one more specialized literary group? Besides, I've loved Pratchett ever since I read his novel about a Discworld newspaper with, due to a misprint, the perfect motto: "The Truth Will Make You Fret."

NEW AND OLD

The other day a friend casually remarked that most of the books in what might be called my library probably came to me as freebies. I answered that that wasn't true at all, that perhaps 10 percent had originated as review copies. In fact, just this morning, while groggily sipping my morning coffee, I scanned the nearest bookcase — built by yours truly some 30 years ago — and realized that on its six shelves, containing perhaps 150 books, only four of them weren't purchased with my cold hard credit card.

Which four, you ask? The opening quartet of Patrick O'Brian's Jack Aubrey-Stephen Maturin series. In fact, Norton sent me the entire uniform set, back when I reviewed *The Commodore.* (That novel, by the way, mentions a small boat called the *Ringle,* its name immortalizing Ken Ringle, a former *Washington Post* colleague and ardent sailor, who told O'Brian about Chesapeake Bay skipjacks.) The subsequent 15 volumes are in storage. To display them all would take up too much space, so I just keep out the early ones, against the day I might want to reimmerse myself in the salty waters of the Aubrey-Maturin adventures.

Before I came to Washington, I could fit all my books — and all my clothes, indeed everything I then owned — into a 1966 fire-engine red Chevy Impala. But once I arrived in our nation's capital, I quickly discovered that the place bulged with secondhand books. With my friend David Streitfeld, now with *The New York Times,* I once visited every used bookstore in the metro area as part of a story for the *Washington Post*'s Weekend section. There were something like 60 all told. On top of this, there were gigantic annual book sales — Vassar, Brandeis, and Stone Ridge, in particular — and church sales and antiquarian book fairs and thrift shops and even people selling old books from blankets on the sidewalk. I once bought some novels by Carl Van Vechten from just such a guy, after noticing that all the books he displayed were by authors whose names began with V. He told me that when Loudermilk's bookstore closed down, the fiction was auctioned off by letter and the hot letters — F and W, for instance — were out of his price range.

Before long, I was hammering together one wooden bookcase after another. Two years later my Macomb House apartment, around the corner from the Washington zoo, was lined with books, floor to ceiling. At least then everything was on a shelf, which is more than I can say today.

In those pre-Internet days, each week the postman would deliver one or two book catalogues. Mail-order houses, specialty dealers, remainder outlets, the Strand in New York — once you were on the mailing lists, many happy evenings could be spent sipping a glass of wine and checking off the titles of the books you'd like to buy, if only you had a bit more money. At some point, I even subscribed to *AB Bookman's Weekly,* the journal of the secondhand trade, each issue proffering an article or two, a bit of publishing news, ads from dealers around the country highlighting new acquisitions, and, not least, a couple of dozen pages devoted to Books Wanted and Books for Sale.

Mostly I just daydreamed about all these out-of-reach treasures. One fateful afternoon, however, I finally screwed up my courage and actually ordered a collection of stories from the bookseller (and sf/fantasy author) Nelson Bond: it was *Brass Knuckles,* by Frank Gruber. Gruber was one of the 1930s *Black Mask* boys; his memoir *The Pulp Jungle* is fairly well known. Along with his hard-boiled fiction, though, he also produced a lighthearted series about Oliver Quade, a reference-book salesman who had memorized the encyclopedia and used his arcane knowledge to solve crimes. I'd read one or two of these Human Encyclopedia stories as a boy and loved them. *Brass Knuckles* collects them all and whatever I paid, it was cash well spent.

Soon I was buying books pretty readily, though I was still my mother's son: a bargain-hunter. Then one day a catalogue arrived featuring a coveted title priced at the outrageous sum of $15. It was a first edition of Randall Jarrell's *A Sad Heart at the Supermarket.* Back at college I had read to pieces my paperback of Jarrell's famous collection *Poetry and the Age.* This was his second book of essays, one that had never been issued in softcover. Naturally, I had to have it, so I swallowed hard, sent Quill & Brush a check, and received back a small substantial package. When I finally made my way through multiple layers of padding and plastic wrap, I noticed that my new treasure's dj was encased in some kind of protective cellophane or mylar. I soon learned that dust jackets, being fragile and susceptible to tears, needed their own jackets.

I read the Jarrell almost immediately — many of its pages lament the decline of reading — and the following weekend decided to visit Quill & Brush, then located in Olney, Maryland. Its genial owners, Allen and Pat Ahearn, told me how they had begun acquiring firsts back in their college days at the University of Maryland, eventually opening this shop. Allen worked at the Pentagon from Monday through Friday; Pat took care of their four kids; together they sold books on weekends, specializing in literary first editions. It was Allen who informed me that there were three important points to remember when buying a collectible book: condition, condition, condition.

Any wise collector who lives by that mantra will likely end up with a valuable library. But who can love and then be wise? Looking around this house, I seem to have opted for quantity over quality. Yet I should have known better, given that I eventually worked for Allen and Pat. When Quill & Brush moved to Bethesda, the Ahearns wanted to stay open at least one weekday evening, but who would mind the store? Why, who better than that nice young man with such a passion for books? So for six months, on Thursday from 6 till 9, I dusted the bookcases, filled a few back orders, occasionally even sold something. Naturally, I worked for trade-credit and when traffic was slow, which it usually was, took to wandering among the shelves, pulling out titles, and slowly building up an understanding of "values."

Thus, when one day in another bookstore I spotted a first of Robert Penn Warren's *All the King's Men,* in a fine dust jacket and priced at $50, I didn't hesitate to plunk down what was for me an ungodly sum. I knew the book was worth at least 10 times that. Today it would sell for several thousand dollars.

I know that because I just checked on AbeBooks. Since the rise of the Internet and sites like Abe and AddALL, book bargains are much harder to find, while titles once thought scarce have turned out to be fairly plentiful. Now, you can easily acquire almost anything with a keystroke, if you have the funds. But where's the fun of that? Where's the serendipity? The thrill of the hunt? As Terry Belanger, the retired head of

Charlotteville's Rare Book School, ruefully remarked: that's not collecting, that's shopping.

Well, yes and no. These days I tend to buy rather arcane books, usually older works of popular fiction from roughly 1870 to 1935. In the past I might have had to spend years searching for those titles in brick-and-mortar shops or hoped that someone would respond to my "Books Wanted" ad in *AB Bookman's Weekly.* But in 2012 I can acquire what I need for various projects with relative ease and speed. Even Quill & Brush — relocated to the Ahearns' home on Sugarloaf Mountain — now sells mainly online and through catalogues, only being open to the public by special arrangement. What's more, most of their prices now start at $100. One thing never does change: the books you really covet always cost more than you want to pay for them. But, to borrow a phrase that women use of childbirth, the pain quickly vanishes when you finally hold that longed-for baby, or book, and know that it is yours forever.

DIRTY PICTURES

This past weekend I spent a too-short hour in the National Gallery of Art wandering through a big retrospective exhibition devoted to George Bellows (1882–1925). Bellows is most commonly remembered today for his paintings of boxers, including a famous one of Jack Dempsey being knocked out of the ring. There's also a fairly well known picture called *Forty-Two Kids,* depicting a troop of naked boys swimming and diving off a wharf — I first saw it as an illustration for one of Walt Whitman's poems.

Wonderful as these are, I was most taken with Bellows's urban landscapes and street scenes. He depicts the titanic excavations for New York's Penn Station, huffing laborers on the Hudson River docks, parks filled with snow, the skeletal girders of skyscrapers, carnivalesque tenements, and the whole hurdy-gurdy world that was early 20th-century Manhattan. Bellows also contributed uplifting cover illustrations to *The Masses,* the almost legendary socialist magazine. In his early days he comes across as very much a social-realist painter.

Years ago, when I thought I might one day collect prints, I was drawn to etchings and engravings depicting factories, steel mills, and other industrial sites. There's something about slag heaps and rusting ironworks that just makes my soul sing. I've even been known to admire the ravaged, lunar landscapes created by quarries and strip-mining.

Most obviously, my fondness for foundries and blighted terrains goes back to my hometown Lorain, its one-time motto being "Industrial Empire in Ohio's Vacationland." That vacationland, believe it or not, would be the shores of polluted Lake Erie, not far from Cleveland, where — notoriously — the Cuyahoga River once caught on fire because of the oily chemical slick floating on its waters.

When I was growing up, daily existence in Lorain was dominated by the National Tube division of U.S. Steel, the American Shipbuilding corporation, Thew Shovel, and a Ford assembly plant. As a result, my notions of grandeur and the sublime were shaped by views of smokestacks and half-built lake freighters and diesel cranes stretching their long steel necks toward the sky. The men who worked in these mills and factories — my father and uncles and cousins — were tough, self-reliant, and, to my childish eyes, almost heroic. These guys could fix a car, build a garage, lay bricks, install plumbing, wire a house, raise a garden, hunt and trap and fish and drink and play cards and go to church on Sunday. I, by contrast, always had my nose in a book and now sit in a chair all day while my lily-white fingers type out words on a screen. Sometimes I feel ashamed at how far I've fallen short of the omnicompetence of the hard, quiet men I grew up with.

When I first arrived in Washington I was shocked to see that this city was, and is, the reverse of my hometown. Here people put on a coat and tie to go to work during the week and on Sunday slouch around in jeans and flannel shirts. In Lorain, people wore old, patched clothes to work and saved their good outfits for the weekend. "Sunday best" wasn't just a phrase. Unless they were helping a relative with some big, dirty project, come Sunday my father and mother always wore something "dressy," as did their sullen children, just in case relatives came calling in the afternoon.

One reason I live in Silver Spring, Maryland, is that — before the urban development of recent years — it used to be the sort of place you would go if you needed some spot welding done, where you might buy a cheap wig, or have a muffler replaced, or visit an old-style junk shop. The place had character. Its downtown felt real to me in a way that most of marbled Washington, pretentious Potomac, and the traffic nightmare called Northern Virginia never have. Some of the old Silver Spring still survives, but it is passing quickly.

As they age, most painters grow deeper, more introspective, and often weirder in the way they apply paint or see the world. But in Bellows's case, the opposite occurred. His late work is much weaker — wan and pallid and over-finished and conventional — compared to the muscular energy and boldness of his youthful achievements. Some of the figures in those early paintings look like Boschian grotesques, others scarcely have any face at all. His World War I propaganda paintings of the Hun are truly shocking, including depictions of naked men and women about to be executed. But many of the paintings he did after 1920 when he moved to Woodstock, New York, look like magazine illustrations and sometimes were. Alas, I forgot to notice the dates for his portraits, several of which — notably one of a young girl, lent by the Butler Art Institute of Youngstown, Ohio, where my wife grew up — are as good as anything by John Singer Sargent.

So, the Bellows show was quite wonderful, and yet slightly worrisome too. Artists, and that includes writers, like to think that they get better as they grow older. But sometimes we kid ourselves and that just isn't so. Our youthful ambition and originality disappear, replaced by a boring and bland smoothness, usually dubbed mature professionalism. By contrast, I'm sure that my father and uncles didn't always know how to do a lot of what they did around the house, but, being unable to afford plumbers, roofers or mechanics, they slowly — by trial and error, supplemented by some creative swearing — gradually figured out how to do it themselves. I, of course, just write exorbitant checks to skilled people who come to the house in vans or panel trucks.

It's an old chestnut to say that we need to keep challenging ourselves throughout life. Samuel Beckett memorably declared, "Try again. Fail again. Fail better," while T. S. Eliot proclaimed that "Old men ought to be explorers." More bluntly, Cyril Connolly maintained that we should cast aside whatever "piece of iridescent mediocrity" we are wasting our time with and get down to creating a masterpiece.

Sigh. All of which means that I really should take another stab at writing that novel. Maybe tomorrow.

GOING, GOING, GONE

On any given day I'm likely to be working here at home, hunched over this keyboard, typing Great Thoughts and Beautiful Sentences — or so they seem at the time, like those beautifully flecked and iridescent stones one finds at the seashore that gradually dry into dull gray pebbles. Anyway, I'll be working steadily along when suddenly, as D. H. Lawrence remarked at the beginning of *Sea and Sardinia,* there "comes over one an absolute necessity to move."

I'll then hop into the car and drive to the Friends of the Montgomery County Library bookstore in Wheaton or the Second Story Books Warehouse in Rockville or Wonder Book and Video in Frederick. I'll poke around. Time will pass. And three hours later I'll realize that, oops, I really need to get back home to check over the proof of a review, or reheat some leftovers — I'm no cook — before my Beloved Spouse comes wearily trudging through the backdoor. Yet by the time I pull out of the bookstore's parking lot it is almost invariably rush hour and I will inch painfully along the clotted roadways of greater Washington, frustrated that I should live in this hellhole.

But, ah, those three hours or so of wandering the shelves, pulling out interesting-looking titles, checking prices, trying to remember if I already own this book or that and, if I do, whether I really owe it to myself to upgrade to an incredibly pretty copy for only $5. Before long, my one or two books is a stack, then a boxful. Should I, perhaps, put back a few? Naaah. You only live once. Besides, with any justice, Heaven itself will resemble a vast used bookstore, with a really good café in one corner, serving coffee and Guinness and kielbasa to keep up one's strength while browsing, and all around will be the kind of angels usually found in Victoria's Secret catalogs. All my old friends will be there and sometimes we'll take off a few millennia for an epic poker game and. . . .

To continue: it's true that even $5 book purchases do add up. Yet what, after all, is money? It's just this abstraction, a number, a piece of green paper. But a book — a printed volume, not some pixels on a screen

— is real. You can hold it in your hand. Feel its heft. Admire the cover. Realize that you now own a work of art that is 50 or 75 or 100 years old. Bernard Berenson is, on a grander scale, any collector's *semblable* and *frère*.

Not that I have BB's gift for periodically raking in millions of *lire* by "authenticating" a Giorgione or Tintoretto for art dealer Joseph Duveen. In fact, my Beloved Spouse constantly berates me for failing to stew sufficiently about money. When she tells me to send in my quarterly taxes or deposit cash in my IRA, I do as she says — I am nothing if not uxorious — or I work really hard to accumulate the savings so that I can do so ASAP. For 30 years I diligently set aside every extra penny to cover the college educations of my three sons. I paid off my home mortgage long ago. I even have some kind of mutual fund.

Nonetheless, it's hard for me to feign even mild interest in investing or studying the stock market. What a weary, stale, flat, and unprofitable — okay, make that profitable — way of life it is to think constantly about the bottom line. Keogh plans, Roths, Schedule C, deferred income, capital gains, and rows and rows of little numbers. . . . The heart sinks.

Sometimes I try to care, I really do. But show me an old issue of *Weird Tales* and the latest Bank of America Annual Report, and you'll see where my eyes turn. Of course, both publications deal in fiction, but the lies of art are more honorable than those of plutocratic and deceitful scuzzbags. (Ah, freedom of speech — you got to love it!)

Still, I'm an American, and so can't help but sometimes wish I were lolling in the "one percent." But for me, the cost of even trying to become rich is just too high. Some people can balance the two cultures, artists like Picasso or writers like science fiction's Robert Silverberg who are able to keep track of their portfolios while also creating moving works of art. Sad to say, such multitasking, any multitasking, is beyond me. I read one book at a time all the way through. If I'm reviewing a novel or biography, I then have to write the review before I start my next project. I particularly hate any interruption to what one might laughably call my train of thought. After all, my trains of thought don't precisely resemble the Acela skimming along to New York so much as the Little Engine That Could huffing and puffing up a steep incline.

Most days I'm irrationally content simply

turning pages and fingering keyboards. Essayist Logan Pearsall Smith — Berenson's brother-in-law — once remarked, "People say that life is the thing, but I prefer reading." I wouldn't go that far. As Chaucer's wife of Bath remarked,

> But, Lord Crist! whan that it remembreth
>   me
> Upon my yowthe and on my jolitee,
> It tikleth me aboute myn herte roote.
> Unto this day it dooth myn herte boote
> That I have had my world, as in my tyme.

As I say, even now when I grow foggy-headed or restless, I still hop right into that car of mine and ride around the world — they call me the wanderer, yeah, the wanderer, I roam around, around, around. . . . Hmm, I seem to have flashed backed there to the '60s. Dion on the radio, that night in the Admiral King High School parking lot with. . . . Sigh.

Truth be told, I know I should be more mature and think seriously about my future and make better preparations for whatever dark days await. Naïvely, though, I keep hoping there won't be any really dark days. My ideal farewell to this wicked, wonderful world of books and art and beauty and people was long ago summed up by Edmund Wilson in *To the Finland Station,* his superb account of 19th-century socialism. Its greatest chapter is titled "Karl Marx Dies at His Desk." That's the way to go.

CASTLES IN SPACE

The other day, while roaming through the book-sale room at a local library, I spotted eight or nine issues of *The Magazine of Fantasy and Science Fiction*. All of them were from the early 1960s, with the muted, matte covers of that era, most of them with illustrations by the late Ed Emsh (whose wife, Carol Emshwiller, is one of the greatest living writers of fantasy and sf). Each digest originally cost 40 cents, but now — 50 years later — they were only a quarter apiece, and I bought them all.

For me, such magazines resemble Proust's madeleines: they are vehicles of sweet memory, bibliophilic time machines. An old joke goes: What is the golden age of science fiction? Answer: 12. Back in 1960, when the earliest of these issues of *F&SF* first appeared, I would have been 12. The 1950s and '60s weren't just the heyday of science fiction digests. Corner drugstore racks were crowded with weekly or monthly issues of *Life, True, Mad, Sixteen, The Saturday Review, The Saturday Evening Post, Modern Romance, True Confessions, Reader's Digest, Popular Mechanics,* and *Ellery Queen's Mystery Magazine,* among many others. People read a lot of periodicals in those days. Not anymore. These are especially tough times for genre fiction, even though the magazine short story has always been its best showcase.

Presented for your consideration, as Rod Serling used to say in his introduction to *The Twilight Zone,* the contents of these eight issues of *F&SF.* I count at least four modern classics: Theodore Sturgeon's novella "When You Care, When You Love," Avram Davidson's "The Sources of the Nile," Ray Bradbury's "Death and the Maiden," and Joanna Russ's "My Dear Emily." The incomparable John Collier — best known for his collection *Fancies and Goodnights,* currently available as a New York Review Books paperback — is represented by a novelette "Man Overboard" and Robert Sheckley, whose funniest and most imaginative stories are also available in a volume from NYRB, contributes "The Girls and Nugent Miller." There are also science articles by Dr. Isaac Asimov, book reviews from Damon Knight and Alfred Bester (author of that most seminal of modern sf novels, *The Stars My Destination*), even some examples of light verse by Brian Aldiss, not to overlook the silly punning stories of "Ferdinand Feghoot."

Yet there are lots of real surprises here too. In the September 1960 issue appears "Goodbye," described as the first published story of Burton Raffel. Raffel would make his name not as a pulp fictioneer but as one of the world's most versatile and admired translators, with a special interest in epic works such as *The Nibelungenlied, The Divine Comedy,* and *Don Quixote.* In other issues I find a reprint of Truman Capote's "Master Misery," stories by such largely mainstream authors as George P. Elliott, Howard Fast, and Bruce Jay Friedman, and even an early work by one of my favorite people, that luminary of Wesleyan University, Kit Reed. Given a weekend at the beach, with no looming deadlines, I could be quite happy just reading my two dollars worth of *The Magazine of Fantasy and Science Fiction.* Even the classified ads are redolent of a now-vanished whizbang era. "Develop a powerful mind while asleep. Also, reduce tension, stop smoking, lose weight without drugs. Clinical tests 92% effective. Join International Research group . . . details free." Now what could this be? A come-on for Dianetics? A course in self-induced hypnotism? There's no way to know, except to write in for those free details. Another ad advertises "rocket fuel chemicals" and still another "Birth Control, 34 methods explained" — and not only explained: "Illustrated. $2.98."

The back covers of several issues carry endorsements of the magazine's quality from such literary eminences of the day as Clifton Fadiman and Orville Prescott, not to mention Hugo Gernsback (after whom the famous sf award, the Hugo, is named). Even Louis Armstrong turns out to be a fan: "I believe *The Magazine of Fantasy and Science Fiction* appeals to me because in it one finds refuge and release from everyday life." Unfortunately, the great jazzman goes on: "We are all little children at heart and find comfort in a dream world, and these episodes in the magazine encourage our building castles in space." I don't think any modern sf writers or readers would agree with those saccharine sentiments. And yet, what I'm describing here is exactly that: the comfort found in a dream world.

Today *The Magazine of Fantasy and Science Fiction* is overseen by my friend Gordon Van Gelder, and it's still great. You should try an issue. As it happens, I will be picking up a few more golden-age digests this weekend at Capclave, the local Washington, D.C., science fiction convention, where — as its motto proclaims — "reading is not extinct."

But let me end with a story. A few years ago Elaine Showalter, long a distinguished professor of English at Princeton, retired to Washington. One afternoon we had lunch in Bethesda, and somehow science fiction came up in the conversation. Laughingly, she said that she once taught a student who told her that he had yearned nearly all his life to become the editor of *The Magazine of Fantasy and Science Fiction*. She couldn't quite place his name. I quietly said, "Was it, by chance, Gordon Van Gelder?" With a look of astonishment, she said, "Why, yes. How did you know?" When I told her that Gordon had, in fact, become editor of *F&SF,* she said, and I agreed, "How wonderful to be able to realize the dream of one's life." Happily, some dreams turn out to be more than just castles in space.

Waving, Not Drowning

People sometimes think that I bring home all these old books because I'm addicted, that I'm no better than a hoarder with a houseful of crumbling newspapers. There may be a little truth in this view, one sometimes enunciated by my Beloved Spouse when she's feeling less than pleased with me. Moreover, I do drop by the special biblioholics meeting whenever I attend Readercon, the science fiction convention I wrote about in an earlier column.

But the deeper truth of the matter is somewhat different. All these ziggurats of books in the bedroom and on the attic steps and on top of the piano are future projects, awaiting that time when the stars are finally right. Then great Cthulhu will rise. . . . No, that's something else that happens when the stars are right. As I meant to say, each stack will sooner or later be transformed into an essay, article, or long review.

For instance, just behind me are a half dozen books by or about Julian Maclaren-Ross, a hard-drinking, elegantly raffish bohemian of postwar London who wrote comic novels (*Of Love and Hunger* is about a vacuum cleaner salesman), parodies, short stories, and a volume of reminiscences titled *Memoirs of the Forties.* Paul Willetts helped bring his work back into print, first with a biography — *Fear and Loathing in Fitzrovia* — and then with new editions of the principal works. Maclaren-Ross is, by the way, a model for X. Trapnel in Anthony Powell's 12-part *A Dance to the Music of Time.*

Who are some of the other authors I long to write about? Well, on the landing in the attic sits a box of the Chicago bookman Vincent Starrett's fiction and nonfiction, both waiting for my attention. I owe a Canadian publisher, improbably called the Battered Silicon Dispatch Box, an introduction to Starrett's *Born in a Bookshop.* I've somehow accumulated all of the novels of Elizabeth Taylor — the English writer, not the actress — as well as Nicola Beauman's biography, and one day would like to read them. All I know is that Taylor is frequently likened to Barbara Pym, which is good enough recommendation for me. A couple of years back I enjoyed Sylvia Townsend

Warner's correspondence with her *New Yorker* editor, William Maxwell, and now I seem to own a dozen of her books and feel, quite sheepishly, that I should have started on *Lolly Willowes* and *Mr. Fortune's Maggot* long ago.

Then there's Gerald Kersh, a versatile novelist still known for *Night and the City,* but whose macabre short stories, such as "Men Without Bones" and "The Queen of Pig Island," are horrifically unforgettable. I've found good copies of *Fowlers End* and several of his other works. A step down in literary quality, but a step up in one-time popularity is Dennis Wheatley. Wheatley's thrillers featured aristocratic good guys in battle with Satanic forces, those forces generally seeking to use beautiful young women in Black Masses or other hideous rituals. His most famous book is *The Devil Rides Out,* closely followed by *To the Devil — a Daughter.* Great stuff, plus there's a terrific biography of the man himself by Phil Baker.

Is that all? By no means. That wisest of all science fiction writers, Barry Malzberg, recently suggested that I return to the work of Walter Tevis, whose two most celebrated novels became even more celebrated movies: *The Hustler* and *The Man Who Fell to*

Earth. My friend the late Tom Disch once told me that Tevis's *The Queen's Gambit* — about an abused girl who discovers a profound talent for chess — was the best book he'd ever read about what it must feel like to be a genius.

As you can tell, I do like to listen to my friends and follow their advice. Brian Taves, an authority on early film, P. G. Wodehouse, and Jules Verne, is also an expert on the adventure novels of Talbot Mundy. He generously gave me a few reprints, and I've now bought several more, most recently an old first of *The Nine Unknown.* One day I will sit down and read *Om: The Secret of Ahbor Valley, King of the Khyber Rifles, Jimgrim,* and maybe even the massive *Tros of Samothrace.*

We're not done yet, far from it. I own the four thrillers by Clayton Rawson about the magician-detective The Great Merlini, including *Death from a Top Hat* and *The Footsteps on the Ceiling,* as well as his two short novels about Dan Diavalo. I'm already a fan of the locked-room whodunits of Rawson's friend John Dickson Carr. In fact, the impossible crime has long been my favorite subgenre of the mystery. Of course, it's but the tiniest of steps from the seemingly impossible to the genuinely supernatural, so

I am also fond of psychic detectives and keep meaning to reread, and write something about, William Hope Hodgson's *Carnacki, The Ghost-Finder,* Algernon Blackwood's John Silence stories, Kate and Hesketh Prichard's *The Experiences of Flaxman Low,* and at least one notable contemporary example, *The Collected Connoisseur,* by Mark Valentine and John Howard.

But looking further around the house, I notice all these books by Freya Stark and Lesley Blanch about travels and adventures in the Middle East. I've got half a bookcase devoted to classic accounts of famous murders and notable British and American trials, including F. Tennyson Jesse on Madeleine Smith, Edmund Pearson on Lizzie Borden, William Roughead on Oscar Slater and many others, as well as four or five books by Rayner Heppenstall on the famous criminals of France. Last year David Bellos — biographer and translator of Georges Perec — sent me a copy of his life of Romain Gary, after which I began to pick up the novels of this former husband of both Lesley Blanch and actress Jean Seberg. One of these days I aim to set down my thoughts about time-travel stories, so I own seven or eight collections of these. Having serendipitously found a box of Dornford

Yates's clubman adventures at a yard sale, I eagerly await the right holiday to enjoy *Berry and Co., Jonah and Co., Perishable Goods,* and perhaps a few others. Oh yes, and I've also promised myself to read more of the works of Shakespeare's great contemporary Ben Jonson.

Above all, though, I've accumulated lots of popular fiction from the period between 1875 and 1930. I still occasionally mull over my proposed project for a massive study called "The Great Age of Storytelling." So there are short story collections here by May Sinclair and Marjorie Bowen, lost-race novels such as Cutcliffe Hyne's *The Lost Continent* and Gilbert Collins's *The Stark-enden Quest,* the principal swashbucklers of Stanley Weyman. And so much more. Much, much more.

Sigh. Perhaps my Beloved Spouse is right. While there's definitely method to my madness, it may well be madness nonetheless.

OBERLIN

Over the past few weeks I've found myself thinking a lot about Oberlin College, my alma mater. During the National Book Festival weekend, held on DC's Mall in late September, I spent much of the gala on Friday night with novelist Marilynne Robinson. One of the pieces in her most recent essay collection, *When I Was a Child I Read Books,* is actually entitled "Who Was Oberlin?" (The short answer: John Frederick Oberlin was a saintly, civic-minded preacher in 19th-century Alsace.) Turns out that Robinson is a great admirer of those small, theologically grounded colleges that sprung up during the early-to-mid-19th century, and were led, as in the case of Oberlin, by men such as Charles G. Finney, the most electrifying speaker of his time. Portraits show a man with piercing eyes that really do seem to bore into your soul. Because of the strong convictions of its founders, Oberlin College became our country's first coeducational institution of higher learning and the first to admit both black and white students. The place was, of course, a hotbed of abolitionist sentiment. The social and political activism of Oberlin in the 1960s — my era — grew from more than 100-year-old roots.

On Saturday at the book festival I got to talking with Tony Horwitz, whose latest book is *Midnight Rising: John Brown and the Raid that Sparked the Civil War.* He reminded me that many, if not most, of the men who rode with John Brown had graduated from or had connections with my old school. I actually knew this from having reviewed, a decade or more ago, Nat Brandt's provocatively titled *The Town That Started the Civil War.* Brandt's book focuses not just on Oberlin as an abolitionist stronghold and a stop on the Underground Railroad, but also describes in detail the 1858 "Wellington Rescue," a key event in the lead-up to the Civil War, in which a band of Oberlinians marched to an adjoining village to free an escaped slave from bounty hunters.

Oberlin, I once remarked, fosters two kinds of people: artists and activists. My middle son, Mike, who graduated from the college in 2009, occasionally still wears a beloved T-shirt that reads: "Oberlin: Where dirty, crunchy hippies go to frolic." At the same time, few if any liberal-arts colleges produce more graduates who go on to earn PhDs than this small institution, located — as the jokes have it — either in an Ohio cornfield or "somewhere in the middle of nowhere."

I can remember when I first became aware of the college, or, to be more exact, of its celebrated sister institution, the Oberlin Conservatory of Music. One day at Admiral King High School, in Lorain, Ohio, the students were ordered into the auditorium for an assembly. As my buddies and I sat restlessly in our chairs, probably playing rock-paper-scissors to pass the time, the stage was suddenly invaded by these scruffy older kids in blue jeans and baggy sweat-shirts. They looked like 20th-century versions of the ragtag street urchins Sherlock Holmes used to employ, except that they strode across the polished wood of the stage carrying violins and clarinets, lugging cellos and French horns. After some momentary confusion, the group sat down on folding chairs, placed some sheet music on metal stands, and, with a nod, began to play the most beautiful music I had ever heard.

Many, many years later I got to know the

pianist Eugene Istomin and his wife, Mar-
tita (whose first marriage had been to the
very elderly Pablo Casals). At a particularly
ritzy dinner party I remember telling Eugene that what I loved about Oberlin was
the easy availability of music, the way it was
integrated into one's daily life. Student
recitals at Warner Concert Hall might start
at 7 or 7:30, so one could drop by on the
way to Carnegie Library, slump in a seat,
and listen to a friend play a Beethoven piano
sonata, then go on to study for a couple of
hours. You didn't need to buy a ticket
(except for the special visiting artists series),
and you could wear flip-flops and a raggedy
sweatshirt if you wanted.

Eugene could see my point, but objected.
The way to show one's respect for musi-
cians, he said, was to dress up. Slovenliness
was a sign that the music wasn't worth any
effort. I could, in my turn, understand his
argument, and these days I do put on a dark
suit and tie when attending a concert. But,
now, alas, the cost of tickets, the trouble of
getting downtown and parking, and a dislike for going out at night combine to make
those concerts few and far between. Instead
I listen to CDs and old records. But at
Oberlin I must have heard live music virtually every day. Even the pianos in dorm

lounges were constantly in use, as show tunes and Gilbert and Sullivan rang through the hallways.

Our age, said Emerson, is retrospective. Certainly, Oberlin has been on my mind lately, but not just because of Robinson and Horwitz. A week ago there arrived in the mail a gigantic photographic album titled *Oberlin,* which offers a pictorial homage to my old school. Daguerreotypes and digital photos share many oversized pages. Some of the scenes pictured I remember all too well: the silent vigils in Tappan Square during the Vietnam War, the protesters surrounding the car of a military recruiter. Most make me ache to be 19 again: Here are entire classes lounging under the trees on a spring afternoon, distinguished guest lecturers on the stage at Finney Chapel, painted messages adorning the big rocks across from the old Co-Op Bookstore, the lighted shop front of Gibson's Bakery, blankets of snow covering the streets of the city and campus, the neon sign of the Apollo movie theater, rows and rows of Steinway pianos in the conservatory, the façade of Allen Memorial Art Museum (designed by Cass Gilbert, with a modern addition by Robert Venturi), Claes Oldenburg's giant three-way plug, pretty girls carrying bookbags, the farmland outside the city limits.

It's an excellent photo album, even if — Obies are nothing if not critical — it could have been better. I would have liked more text, more pictures of teachers, more testimonials from notable alumni, though there is an excellent tribute from screenwriter William Goldman. I've just finished reading a biography of Thornton Wilder, which reminded me that the future author of *Our Town* attended Oberlin for two years and that his best friend there was Robert Maynard Hutchins, later the almost legendary president of the University of Chicago. Wilder said that in an education that embraced many schools and universities, including Yale and Princeton, he had had one truly great teacher: Oberlin's Professor of English Charles Wager.

You probably haven't heard of Wager, unless you are connected to the college in some way. Recently, I did pick up the two volumes of his casual essays, largely drawn from the Oberlin alumni magazine and collected under the title *To Whom It May Concern*. In my undergraduate days I wrote chunks of my honors thesis — on the poetry of William Empson — in the Wager Seminar Room of Carnegie Library. Still Wager's influence on me was quite profound, in the indirect but typical way of academia: I took a class on 17th-century metaphysical poetry from his protegé, the quietly formidable Andrew Bongiorno. He, too, like so many Oberlin teachers before and since, poured his energies into teaching, rather than swanning about as a "public intellectual."

Readers familiar with my memoir *An Open Book* know that Oberlin College dramatically changed my life. For a decade after I graduated, hardly a day went by when I didn't imagine that I would eventually return there to teach, live in one of those big Victorian houses on Morgan Street, become, in fact, a professor just like Bongiorno and Wager. I have fallen short of that dream. Still, if I were ever, like Emily in *Our Town,* permitted to relive one day of my checkered past, I would choose a beautiful October afternoon in Oberlin, when all the world was young.

JACQUES BARZUN — AND OTHERS

Last week, the distinguished cultural historian, teacher, and man of letters Jacques Barzun died at the age of 104. For a while there, it seemed that Barzun — rhymes approximately with "parson" — might go on forever, adding to our knowledge of the past, assailing the decline of standards, both exemplifying and fighting for cultured, civilized values. Certainly up through his 90s, he remained active as a scholar and writer, even producing a surprise best seller, *From Dawn to Decadence: 500 Years of Western Cultural Life,* in 2000, when he was 92.

This past year Michael Murray brought out *Jacques Barzun: Portrait of a Mind,* tracking his subject's astonishing life from a French boyhood in which Barzun played marbles with the poet Guillaume Apollinaire through a brilliant career at Columbia University, first as an undergraduate, then as a teacher, and finally as the university's provost. Murray relates a particularly delightful story about young Professor Barzun. In one of his first history classes, Barzun recalled, there "was a beautifully dressed man of about forty, with very black hair and a signet ring with a diamond and a tie pin; he was done up to the nines. At the end of the first semester, he came to me and said: 'I am a Turk, and I want to express my gratitude because in your dealing with the Turkish question you have been perfectly fair. This means so much. I want to tell you that if ever at any time someone stands in your way or has done you harm, here is my card, just call me, and he will be taken care of.' "

Barzun then added, "I have strewn the byways with my victims."

Barzun's best-known books include *Berlioz and the Romantic Century*, *Teacher in America*, *A Stroll with William James*, and *Simple and Direct*, a guide to writing. But I've always thought that *A Catalogue of Crime*, written with his lifelong friend Wendell Hertig Taylor, could be his most lasting masterpiece. I keep it by my bedside, along with a handful of similarly wide-ranging and often idiosyncratic reference books, such as E. F. Bleiler's *Guide to*

Supernatural Fiction and Martin Seymour-Smith's *New Guide to Modern World Literature.* All these volumes are dog-eared and marked up, with loosened bindings; booksellers sometimes facetiously describe their condition as "much loved."

My own copy of *A Catalogue of Crime* is certainly "much loved," even though I disagree with many of the book's harsh judgments on modern crime fiction. Barzun and Taylor definitely champion classic whodunits, especially those written with wit, panache, and, above all, cleverness. The *Catalogue* lists more than 5,000 novel-length mysteries, collections of detective stories, true-crime books, and assorted volumes celebrating the delights of detection. Every entry is annotated, and a succinct critical judgment given. For instance, John Dickson Carr's historical reconstruction *The Murder of Sir Edmund Godfrey* is summed up as "a classic in the best sense — i.e., rereadable indefinitely." The brief account of *Murder Plain and Fanciful,* edited by James Sandoe, opens: "This virtually perfect anthology seems never to have been reprinted, which is a disgrace as well as a deprivation to the reading public." The brief description of Dorothy L. Sayers' *Strong Poison* reads as follows in its entirety: "JB puts this highest among the masterpieces. It has the strongest possible element of suspense — curiosity *and* the feeling one shares with Wimsey for Harriet Vane. The clues, the enigma, the free-love question, and the order of telling could not be improved upon. As for the somber opening, with the judge's comments on how to make an omelet, it is sheer genius."

I sometimes like to imagine Barzun spending the first decade of the 21st century reading and rereading his favorite authors, in particular, Arthur Conan Doyle, Rex Stout, and Agatha Christie. He once wrote that Archie Goodwin, the legman for Stout's fat detective Nero Wolfe, was a modern avatar of Huck Finn and one of the most memorable characters in American literature. As a teacher, Barzun taught any number of distinguished writers, from science fiction giant Robert Silverberg to the cultural essayist Arthur Krystal and the award-winning musicologist Jack Sullivan. He was also, of course, a great supporter of, and contributor to, *The American Scholar.* Alas, I never knew him, except through his books.

But I have been lucky enough to meet two other great centenarians of scholarship: M. H. Abrams and Daniel Aaron. Abrams taught at Cornell, where, in another life, I earned a Ph.D. in comparative literature. He retired a year after I got there, so I only knew him very casually and wasn't able to take any of his classes. His masterpiece, *The Mirror and the Lamp,* tracks the shift from classicism to romanticism in English poetry. From all reports he remains vigorous, this fall even bringing out a new collection of occasional pieces, *The Fourth Dimension of a Poem and Other Essays.* Daniel Aaron, of Harvard, is one of our most revered Americanists, author of the classic study *Writers on the Left,* editor of Edmund Wilson's letters, co-founder of the Library of America, and famous for riding his bicycle all around Cambridge well into his 90s.

When I first began to work as an editor at *The Washington Post Book World* back in the late 1970s, it was my habit to ask quite elderly writers and scholars to review for me. My secret reason for this was simply to connect, however briefly, through letter, telephone call, or handshake, with these eminent men and women, but also with the great writers who had been their friends and associates. Favorite authors like Scott Fitzgerald, Edmund Wilson, W. H. Auden, and Evelyn Waugh were already dead, but I could reach out to *their* friends, including

Malcolm Cowley, Peter Quennell, Eleanor Clark, Rex Warner, Stephen Spender, Sir Harold Acton, Sir John Pope-Hennessy, Douglas Bush, and many others. Once a retired Boston University professor reviewed two books about T. E. Lawrence, with whom he had done brass rubbings while they were both undergraduates at Oxford. Warren Ault wrote the review at age 102.

These days I occasionally correspond with the great Dostoevsky biographer and critic, and former Princeton and Stanford professor, Joseph Frank, who is in his mid-90s. Just this year, he too brought out a new book, *Responses to Modernity: Essays in the Politics of Culture.* It includes essays on, among others, Paul Valéry, André Malraux, Ernst Jünger, T. S. Eliot, and two of Frank's former colleagues, the critic R. P. Blackmur (of Princeton) and the pioneering scholar of the novel Ian Watt (of Stanford).

Figures like Jacques Barzun — and Abrams, Aaron, and Frank — seem to me the last representatives of a traditional literary scholarship that is now out of fashion. To this group, one might add Victor Brombert and a few octogenarians, such as Abrams's former student Harold Bloom and the comparatist and Bible translator Robert Alter. No doubt there are others I am overlooking. But these academic eminences have all worked hard to become truly learned, and their scholarship is vitalized by a deep knowledge of, and serious engagement with, the great works of the past. Until last week, Jacques Barzun was the oldest, and one of the best, of these living cultural treasures.

What's in a Name?

Early in October I attended Capclave, Washington, D.C.'s annual science fiction convention. Over the course of a long weekend I manfully served on five panels: "*A Princess of Mars'* One-Hundred Year Reign" (2012 is the centennial of Edgar Rice Burroughs's famous first novel); "Classics with Class" (about which I can remember nothing); "Unsung Author" (an ongoing category, this year's focus being the sly, black-humored short-story writer Robert Sheckley); "The Heritage of Edgar Rice Burroughs" (a panel with several Burroughs fans from the National Capital Panthans), and finally "Who Are the Early Masters of Modern Science Fiction?" I was also interviewed for Fast Forward, a long-running series of video conversations with people involved in sf.

In short, I kept pretty busy over the weekend, though not so busy that I couldn't spend some time in the dealers' room, where I bought an Ace Double paperback, consisting of Ron Goulart's *Clockwork's Pirates* and *Ghost Breaker*. It was the latter title I wanted, a humorous collection of stories about the occult detective Max Kearney. The book's come-on line — beneath an illustration featuring a green-tentacled blob, a shapely young woman in nothing but stiletto heels and a bikini bottom, and a Bogart-like figure wearing a slouch hat and trench coat — reads: "Having trouble with psi powers, spooks, or E-T visitations? Take it up with Max Kearny!" (As readers of this feature may recall from a previous column, books featuring occult or psychic detectives — like John Silence and Carnacki, the Ghost-Finder — are a little sideline of my collecting.)

I also bought eight little matchboxes, each imprinted with the first-edition cover of some fantasy or sf classic. Last spring I acquired a couple of these novelties at the Malice Domestic convention — Dashiell Hammett's *The Dain Curse* and Agatha Christie's *Murder on the Orient Express* — and these have now been joined by Ray Bradbury's *The Martian Chronicles*, Olaf Stapledon's *Last and First Men*, Jules Verne's *From the Earth to the Moon*, L. Frank Baum's

The Marvelous Land of Oz, and several others. They look great, like a little row of miniature books, as they face me amid the pencils and postcards, the action figures (Poe, Sherlock Holmes), the Bettie Page tumbler and the photograph of Louise Brooks, the Edward Gorey bookmark, the "Don't Panic" button, various small rocks, and all the other detritus that clutters my desk.

On the Saturday evening of Capclave I went out to dinner with the aforementioned Panthans. This group, affiliated with the national Burroughs Bibliophiles (whose meetings are called Dum-Dums), consists of ardent collectors of, and experts on, the books of ERB. A highlight of one local guy's collection is the original $400 check paid by Munsey publications to Edgar Rice Burroughs for the 1912 magazine serialization of *Under the Moons of Mars,* the original title of *A Princess of Mars.* Another member collects Burroughs trading cards, often depicting scenes from Tarzan comics or reproductions of old paperback covers. Certainly no red-blooded American male of my generation can fail to remember Roy Krenkel and Frank Frazetta's illustrations for the 1960s softcover reissues of the Tarzan and Mars books — if only for the lusciously underclad lovelies such as Dian of Pellucidar and Thuvia, Maid of Mars.

Saturday's dinner was going along pleasantly enough when suddenly a tablemate gasped, laughed, looked up at me, dropped the issue of the *National Capital Panthans Journal* she had in her hand, and said, "You've been tuckerized."

So, finally, I'd been tuckerized. My life was complete.

If you look up "tuckerization" on Wikipedia you will find it succinctly defined as "the act of using a person's name in an original story as an in-joke." (The word derives from Wilson Tucker, the sf writer who named some of his characters after his friends.) These days charity events often feature an auction in which people bid to be "tuckerized" by a favorite author. In effect, this is the equivalent of winning a tiny walk-on part in a TV series or film.

My old *Book World* colleague Michele Slung was the first person I knew whose name was "borrowed" by an author. Michele had enthusiastically reviewed Jonathan Carroll's eerie classic, *The Land of Laughs,* and in Carroll's later book *Bones of the Moon,* a character encounters a mysterious tribe known as The Slung People. At about the same time, another friend, sf reviewer Greg Feeley, was also "tucker-ized," but not quite so pleasantly. A novel-ist, offended by a Feeley review, didn't just shrug it off: in a subsequent book he featured a race of loathsome, subterranean creatures called the Feelies.

In my own case, a group of people — characters in an ongoing Burroughs' pastiche called *Invaders of the Inner World* by Lee Strong — are said to inhabit the Utopian city of Dirda. While it was a kick to find my name in Strong's serial, for a long while I have wondered if Jack Vance, now in his mid-90s and the dean of American fantasy and science fiction writers, didn't somehow possess precognitive knowledge that a critic with my name would love and champion his books. After all, one of Vance's novels bears the title *The Dirdir,* he has a series called *The Durdane Trilogy,* and throughout his vast oeuvre there are several other names surprisingly close to Dirda.

Once upon a time, I started to write an "impossible crime" mystery and decided to give its characters punning monikers: I now only remember a gay guy named Perry Bathhouse (cf. Alexander Pope's essay *Peri Bathous*) and a young woman called Gloria Mundy (*Gloria Mundi*), but there were at least a half dozen other examples of sophomoric wittiness. Since there were already famous P.I.'s named Marlowe and Spenser, I dubbed my detective Dekker, after still another Renaissance writer. Alas, I don't remember much about the story itself, except that the villain — or was it a villain-ess? — had to be absolutely naked to commit a murder and not leave any trace. The modus operandi was, I think even now, quite ingenious. Perhaps it's time I unearthed that manuscript and gave it another look, or, maybe, even finished the story. Start watching the best-seller lists.

LANGUAGE MATTERS

As soon as I decided to write about language for this "Browsings" column, my sentences started to grow clumsy and fall all over one another. Nothing sounded right, and I questioned the grammar and syntax of virtually every clause. Isn't there an old joke about how a bird couldn't fly or a thousand-legger couldn't skitter along once either started to contemplate how the flying or skittering was done?

Like most writers, I confess to a number of linguistic tics and crotchets. While ambiguity seems to me a plus in poetry — I didn't write my honors thesis on William Empson for nothing — it is something I tend to avoid in prose. I try to practice. . . . But wait. Look again at that sentence with the dashes: Shouldn't there be a comma after the word "poetry"? The dashes make that impossible, but in such a case do they render a comma superfluous? Will anyone care besides me?

Not for the first time do I wish that I hadn't disdained the study of grammar when young. Nowadays, I would just recast the above sentence to avoid this punctuational uncertainty, but I'll let it go this time as an example of the kind of linguistic bump that tends to trouble me. Nothing, after all, should interfere with the smooth flow of my mellifluous and pellucid paragraphs.

Or should that be "pellucid and mellifluous paragraphs"? I wrote that as a bit of self-mockery — ironic deflation as a way of deflecting charges of vanity — but I do tend to be leery of alliteration and those two "p" words next to each other give me pause. On the other hand (but where was the first hand?), reversing the order of the adjectives leads to a less pleasing rhythm. What to do? Perhaps being a little jokey is simply a mistake?

Too much consciousness, observed Dostoevsky's Underground Man, is a disease, a positive disease. All writers long to lose themselves in the creative moment, to find themselves caught up in what was once dubbed "the divine afflatus," when the words come trippingly to the tongue and thoughts achieve a profundity that Plato might envy. . . . Oh, dear, I recognize that last analogy as one of my go-to rhetorical tricks. Such and such a quipster is so witty that Oscar Wilde might envy him; a certain stylist is so precise that she could give lessons to Flaubert. The formula strikes me as mildly amusing, but I do it all the time unless I catch myself.

While writers hope their inner daemons will guide their pens, an editor needs the kind of cold clinical intelligence that Sherlock Holmes might learn from. (See what I mean?) When I rewrite — and sometimes I'll spend hours making a piece sound as if it had been tossed off as easily as Byron scribbled his letters — I carefully go over every sentence. (Oops, that same dashes problem again and more of those tiresome analogies.) Somehow, one hopes to achieve a balance, so that the prose all tracks properly but doesn't sound costive, constrained, or too carefully considered. (Hmm, should I change all those "c"s?) Unless you're actually after a Thomas Browne-like oratorical solemnity, you probably want to sound natural, whatever that is. (Note that I've moved from "I" to "One" to "You" in almost as many sentences — that seems wrong, but will anyone notice?)

In fact, this column wasn't really meant to be about my own flaw-specked writing, but about linguistic puzzles and anomalies. Last month, the October issue of *Consumer Reports* carried the headline: "America's Worst Scams." Looking at it, I wondered if that shouldn't be "America's Best Scams"? Really terrible scams wouldn't be particularly effective, would they? I went back and forth on this and still haven't decided.

Or take the expression: "It goes without saying," as in "It goes without saying that Dirda isn't half the writer he thinks he is." If it doesn't need to be said, why does one need to say it? And, to stick with this same sentence, how can anyone know how good a writer I think I am? Personally, I hold a rather low opinion of myself, constantly desiring this man's art and that man's scope. (There's another of my quirks — the buried allusion, the embedded quotation without any identification of the source. Shakespeare, by the way, Sonnet 29.)

A lot of idioms trouble me. Every time I try to use "Notwithstanding" in a sentence, I find myself confused. Should it be "Notwithstanding his sheer brilliance, Dirda is . . ." or, "His sheer brilliance notwithstanding, Dirda is . . ."? I can never decide and so just give it all up and poor Dirda loses his claim to brilliance yet again.

I could go on. I can't go on. I'll go on.

(Beckett, this time.) Just bide with me a little while longer, and we'll soon be done. In my hot youth (Byron, of course), I used to study books such as — or should that be "study such books as"? — Robert Graves and Alan Hodge's *The Reader Over Your Shoulder,* Fowler's *Modern English Usage,* Herbert Read's *English Prose Style,* Bonamy Dobrée's *Modern Prose Style,* Arthur Quiller-Couch's *On the Art of Writing* (Q, as he was known, is the source of the notorious "murder your darlings" rule of writing), Strunk and White's *Elements of Style,* and even G. O. Curme's scholarly *Syntax.* Today, I occasionally dip into an old copy of *The Oxford Book of English Prose,* and often wish I could achieve the grand flights (slight echo there of Wallace Stevens) and Olympian grandiloquence of Gibbon and Ruskin. But Thoreau was my earliest model — as it was E. B. White's — and I seem locked into a plain, homespun style, albeit one gussied up with the borrowed finery (now where's that from?) of pervasive quotation and allusion.

Somerset Maugham used to say — and I've quoted this a dozen times if I've quoted it once — that if a man would write perfectly, he would write like Voltaire. In truth, I'd settle for being able to write like Rousseau or Diderot, or Arthur Machen, Evelyn

Waugh, Cyril Connolly, or Janet Flanner or Joseph Mitchell. I wouldn't want to write like Henry James, though, or Virginia Woolf — too much brocade for my taste. Alas, there seems small likelihood that my style will ever be perceived as other than a poor thing but mine own (Shakespeare, again, slightly skewed).

"I'm Done"

When Philip Roth recently announced his retirement from writing fiction, I was surprised and impressed. Over the years Roth has won all the prizes except the Nobel, and he's been producing bestsellers and critically acclaimed (and controversial) books since he was in his 20s. During the past decade the Library of America has even begun reissuing his complete works in its familiar, stately editions — a nice rounding-off to an enviable career. As Kenny Rogers told us long ago, you've got to know when to hold 'em, when to fold 'em, and when to walk away.

Some years back, I happened to interview John Updike and asked him if there would be more novels about Harry Angstrom — perhaps "Rabbit Resurrected"? — or any more stories featuring the writer Henry Bech. In essence, Updike said no. Those characters' adventures were over, and he himself was now largely focused on "clearing his desk." Updike did keep writing up to the end, but, apart from some moving poetry, most people would agree that his later work added little to his reputation.

Should older writers keep at it until they breathe their last? It's a hard call. Sophocles supposedly brought out *Oedipus at Colonus* when he was in his 80s. The elderly Tolstoy turned himself into an Old Testament prophet, producing cranky attacks on Shakespeare and numerous political and religious tracts. Yet he also wrote *Hadji Murad,* one of his greatest works (and a particular favorite of Harold Bloom).

What must be hard for all established writers of a certain age is seeing the world turn its spotlight elsewhere. Once they were the stars, up front and center, and now other names — sometimes those of their understudies — are in neon at the top of the marquee. Gods that survive too long tend to be taken for granted, ignored or even mocked. How many young people still read John Barth? I can remember the excitement I felt over the linked novellas of *Chimera,* the imaginative experiments of *Lost in the Funhouse.* But when was the last time anyone opened *Giles Goat-Boy*? And yet Barth is an absolutely wonderful and astonishing writer. It's just that the stage now belongs to David Mitchell, Zadie Smith, and the Jonathans Franzen and Safran Foer. But 30 years from now, they, too, will be yesterday's news.

Still, some lucky writers do manage a late flowering. Philip Roth himself reblossomed, after a period of relatively minor work, with *The Human Stain* and *American Pastoral* (and, a favorite of mine, that harrowing novella, *The Dying Animal*). In old age an artist, whether in paint, music, or prose, will sometimes cast aside his usual manner and indulge in some playful romp. Mann brought out his lighthearted paean to the counterfeit in *Confessions of Felix Krull, Confidence Man;* Faulkner produced the rumbustious odyssey of *The Reivers,* Thornton Wilder reimagined his young self as a kind of amateur trouble-solver in *Theophilus North.* In another field, Matisse, though nearly blind, produced his glorious paper cut-outs. These works are distinctly exuberant, even comic, but other late works show us the artist confronting age, the loss of powers, and death. Just look at the final self-portraits of Rembrandt, or listen to Richard Strauss's *Four Last Songs.* The rest is silence.

Old men (and women) ought to be explorers, but mainly they're not. Instead feckless, irresponsible young whippersnappers break the new paths in art and letters (and in other fields too). As the years go by, many aging masters are simply forgotten. Even if they bring out a new book, it will be half-ignored, or people will say, "Is she still writing?" or "I thought he was dead." All those big fat volumes called *Collected Poems* are tombs as much as tomes. *Hic jacet.*

Mentoring is the last refuge of the older artist. With luck, disciples will keep one's books in print, one's reputation alive. Doubtless even the most unassuming poet or novelist can get used to reverence and genuflection. Of course, there remains the possibility of betrayal: Judas writes the biography, that mousey acolyte may turn out to be Eve Harrington (from "All About Eve"). After all, new writers do need to clear a space for themselves, even if it means pushing aside a once-revered elder of the tribe.

And what about "senior" critics? Ah, their fate is the worst of all. They lose touch with the new, start to go on and on about the old days, either turn into literary Kris Kringles or bitter curmudgeons. And then they are, most of them anyway, forgotten altogether. Where now are William Troy and

Vernon Young, Orville Prescott and John Mason Brown, Agnes Repplier, Diana Trilling, and even Mary McCarthy? Once they were powers in the land, their judgments feared and their praise yearned after, but today their names scarcely raise an ironic smile of recognition.

Oh, the House of Fame! Sometimes it is as harsh and cruel a place as Dr. Moreau's House of Pain. What is the law? Literary generations come and go, and each generation passeth away and is heard of no more. In the end, simply the artistic making itself — of poems and stories and essays — delivers the only reward a writer can be sure of. And, perhaps, the only one that matters.

POE AND BAUDELAIRE

This past weekend, I wandered into downtown Silver Spring, Maryland, to attend a book arts festival sponsored by Pyramid Atlantic, a cooperative devoted to teaching and promoting every sort of paper-based art and craft. Part of the two-day festival included printing and papermaking demonstrations at the Pyramid Atlantic studios, as well as lectures by noted local artists. For instance, it was fun to learn how all those wonderfully garish posters — the kind tacked to the sides of telephone poles or kiosks — were designed and produced for visiting carnivals, county fairs, and rock concerts.

Did I mention that there was also a related book fair at the Silver Spring civic center?

As I sauntered among the booths, I noticed that one vendor was selling what she called Mean Cards. Instead of saccharine Hallmark greetings and congratulations, these were inscribed "Just Go Away and Die," "Everyone Hates You," "Jerk," and "You Look Awful. Seriously." When I pointed these out to my Beloved Spouse, that gentle dove immediately bought the entire stock. You don't want to cross Marian Dirda.

I, of course, Mr. Sweetness and Light, continued my usual aimless meandering, pausing to check out the fine-press offerings from Baltimore's Kelmscott Bookshop and to page through various limited editions published in runs of just 200 copies. In short, I was enjoying myself in a quiet, low-keyed sort of way — quiet and low-keyed because almost nothing at the fair seemed quite to my taste.

No matter how beautiful the paper, artwork, printing, and binding, I'm seldom drawn to a book unless it's by a writer I care about or on a subject that appeals to me. Many private press items, however, tend to be of largely regional interest — California history, the journals of some early pioneer, descriptions of the natural world. All worthy subjects and worthy of support, but, as we used to say in the '60s, not my thing. So I felt free and easy under the apple boughs, or rather among the booths, until I came to Bowerbox Press. The proprietor,

Val Lucas, mainly offered a wide supply of cards, handsomely decorated with birds. Ms. Lucas was clearly fascinated by all things avian because she'd also brought along two large woodblock prints, 18 inches by 24: one featured a gull-like seabird in full flight, the other a somewhat sinister crowlike creature.

The seabird first caught my eye, in part because of the bold title: "The Albatross." I then noticed a bit of squared-up text, obviously stanzas, underneath the image. Now there are only two well-known poems that feature an albatross, Coleridge's "Rime of the Ancient Mariner" and "The Albatross" by Baudelaire, in which he compares the artist, mocked and out of place in society, to the seabird, which is comparably clumsy and awkward when not soaring among the clouds. I stooped down to see if the poem was a section of "The Ancient Mariner" or if it might be the Baudelaire. Instinctively, my eyes went to the last line, and I read: "Ses ailes de géant l'empêchent de marcher" — "His giant wings prevent him from walking."

As for the black bird: since it wasn't the Maltese Falcon, it could only be, and was, a raven, with Poe's Halloween classic somewhat tightly printed underneath. I suspect that "Quoth the Raven: 'Nevermore!' " may be the most famous line in American poetry.

"The Albatross" and "The Raven" — studies in light and dark — certainly looked very handsome together. The pair, however, were hardly what you'd call cheap. Neither were they impossibly expensive. Still, with wholly uncharacteristic resolve, I finally walked away. I eventually walked home, too, albeit in a thoughtful mood. And the next day I hurried back to the fair and bought both prints.

It is a truth universally acknowledged that M. Dirda is a sucker for anything bookish in the way of artwork. On the mantel in my living room you will see Leonard Maurer's big etching of James Joyce — another copy used to hang in the offices of *Book World* above art director Francis Tanabe's desk — and Dan Miller's woodblock of W. B. Yeats and Ray Driver's pen-and-ink portrait of Shakespeare as a sleek Broadway-style theatrical impresario. Back in the happy days when I taught and enjoyed an office at McDaniel College, I was able to deck the walls (and shelves) with the following:

A photograph of Borges
A framed postcard of W. H. Auden petting
    a cat

An old publicity shot of M. F. K. Fisher, with her hair sleeked back and looking to-die-for gorgeous

The reproduction of a photograph of bookman Vincent Starrett, with the caption "A cigar and lots of old books — what more could one ask for?"

A high-quality reproduction of a drawing of Ezra Pound by Guy Davenport, in the Easter-Island style of Henri Gaudier-Brzeska

A colored photograph of Chekhov, set in an elaborate frame that I bought at a Russian store in New York

Two Richard Thompson caricatures of T. S. Eliot and Bernard Shaw, drawn in what looks like a soft gray conté crayon

A poster of Tenniel's Caterpillar from *Alice in Wonderland:* "Who are you?"

A framed post card of M. R. James, author of *Ghost Stories of an Antiquary,* seen in profile at his desk

A period-style lobby card for a new translation of Jules Verne's play *Journey Through the Impossible*

A poster advertising the Atlantic Center for the Arts (where I once taught writing and later worked on two of my books)

Lots of small pen-and-ink images, drawn

by the much loved and still-missed Susan Davis as illustrations for my Readings column in *The Washington Post*

Of course, I haven't even mentioned the Sherlockian art or the poster of Bettie Page or the facsimile cover of the first Batman comic. Still, like many of my books, most of this material is stored away in boxes, awaiting the day when I'll wake up and find myself the possessor of a proper library. If I'm lucky, my eyes will still be good enough to read with and my liver will be functioning, so that I'll be able to sprawl in a leather armchair and sip brandy and gaze at these mementos of a bookish life — while listening to Ben Webster or Mozart on the sound system. Where your treasure is, there will your heart be also.

IN PRAISE OF SMALL PRESSES

Books don't only furnish a room, they also make the best holiday gifts. Note that I said "books." Kindles and Nooks and iPads may offer texts, but word-pixels on a screen aren't books. Come Christmas morning, what do you tell your significant other? "Darling, I can't thank you enough for this download of *The Hobbit* for my e-Reader." I don't think so. Somehow, this isn't quite the same as unwrapping a signed first printing of *The Hobbit* in a fine dust jacket (many bucks), or Douglas Anderson's information-packed annotated edition (invaluable), or any of the handsome versions illustrated by Michael Hague or Alan Lee or Tolkien himself.

No, a Christmas present should be, well, something present, right there in your hands after you've read the gift card and ripped aside the ribbons and bows and red-and-green paper decorated with snowmen and Santas.

So hie thee to your nearest bookstore, be it an independent like Washington's Politics and Prose or a big box Barnes & Noble. What could be a better way to shop for the holidays than to spend an hour or two, alone or with your family, looking at books? In my own case, of course, I try to make it Christmas every day, or at least once a week.

All of which said, I want to make a pitch for some works you aren't likely to find in your local bookstore, no matter how extensive its holdings: small-press titles. In recent years, as trade houses increasingly gravitate to wholly commercial "product," specialty publishers and independent presses have risen up to make available wonderful books, real books, of all kinds. Let me stress that I'm not talking about those generic print-on-demand titles, many of which are barebones ugly and little better than photocopies bound in bland paper wraps. Nor am I talking about self-published work, so much in the news these days. No, I'm thinking of legitimate small publishers with a mission to bring neglected authors back into print and to produce the kind of books that dreams are made of.

My own tastes are fairly eclectic, but in recent years I've grown intensely interested in science fiction, fantasy, mysteries, and adventure stories written between roughly 1865 and 1935. This "golden age" of story-telling is being served by a number of presses, all of which host websites where you can purchase their offerings. I'm going to list, in alphabetical order, some of my favorites. Just type their names into your search engine, and you will soon be drooling and counting the dollars in your pocket-book.

— Ash-Tree Press specializes in classic English-language ghost stories and weird tales, with a subsidiary imprint, Calabash Press, that publishes material relating to Sherlock Holmes. Recently, much of their backlist has been made available as e-books, but I still recommend the original editions. Some are out of print, but many are still available. Here you can buy the complete supernatural fiction of Arthur Conan Doyle, Vernon Lee and Sheridan Le Fanu, not to overlook John Meade Falkner's eerie novel *The Nebuly Coat* or M. R. James's memoir *Eton and King's.*

— Centipede Press brings out several kinds of books — oversized portfolios, such as the complete art work of Lee Brown Coye, collections of commentary on influential horror films such as *Carrie,* handsome editions, often illustrated, of classic titles (most recently *Dr. Jekyll and Mr. Hyde*), and the major works of important genre authors. For example, this fall Centipede is offering five volumes devoted to the great noir writer Cornell Woolrich. The edition of *Phantom Lady* comes with a haunting dust jacket by Matt Mahurin, an introduction by Barry N. Malzberg (who was, for a short time, Woolrich's agent), and a gallery of the covers and film posters for the book and the movie based on it.

— Crippen & Landru takes its name from two of the most famous real-life murderers of England and France. The press only publishes story collections, usually gathering together for the first time the best of an author's scattered short fiction. In their "Lost Classics" series you can acquire perfect holiday entertainment from John Dickson Carr, Ellery Queen, T. S. Stribling (Dr. Poggioli), Michael Gilbert, and Vera Caspary (best known for *Laura*). Crippen & Landru doesn't just focus on the dead, however: here are collections by S. J. Rozan, Lawrence Block, and — this fall — Melodie Johnson Howe, whose "Diana Poole" stories are set in Hollywood.

— Gasogene Books/Wessex Press is the major purveyor of books by Arthur Conan Doyle or about Sherlock Holmes. Any fan of Robert Downey Jr., Benedict Cumberbatch, or Jonny Lee Miller should explore the greater world of Sherlockiana, and this is where to start. Gasogene/Wessex has reissued Vincent Starrett's *Private Life of Sherlock Holmes,* an edition of the 1910 stage production of *The Speckled Band,* a 10-volume collection of the entire Holmes canon (annotated by Leslie S. Klinger), Sherlockian pastiches, CDs, and much else.

— Hippocampus Press is to H. P. Lovecraft what Gasogene is to Sherlock Holmes. For Hippocampus, the great scholar of the weird tale, S. T. Joshi, has edited HPL's letters, occasional writings, and fiction. The press has also brought out Joshi's massive, and massively enjoyable, biography of Lovecraft, as well as the horror and science fiction of other important authors, notably Clark Ashton Smith, M. P. Shiel, and Barry Pain. But Hippocampus casts a wide net, and its list also includes the collected poetry of the California "romantic" George Sterling, several journals, and work by outstanding younger talents like Richard Gavin, author of *At Fear's Altar.*

— Night Shade Books struck gold a couple of years ago by publishing Paolo Bacigalupi's *The Wind-Up Girl,* one of the best and most-honored science fiction novels of recent times. While the press brings out work from many new science fiction and fantasy authors, I've long particularly admired Night Shade's single author collections. Here one can find the complete works of William Hope Hodgson (best known for *The Night Land* and *The House on the Borderland*), all the short fiction of Clark Ashton Smith, who wrote a lushly poetic prose of almost hypnotic beauty, and Lord Dunsany's brilliant "club stories" told by Joseph Jorkens, three delicious double-volumes of tall tales about mermaids and ancient curses, unicorns and trips to Mars.

— Tachyon Publications covers the full spectrum of fantasy and science fiction. Interested in steampunk? Here are basic anthologies by Ann and Jeff VanderMeer. Like the work of Kage Baker, author of "The Company" novels? Here are her essays on silent film. A fan of Peter Beagle, Michael Swanwick, James Morrow, Joe R. Lansdale, Tim Powers? Here are some of their best works. Indeed, Tachyon's edition of Powers's *The Bible Repairman and Other*

Stories just won this year's World Fantasy Award for best short-story collection.

— Tartarus Press books are immediately recognizable: Most of the volumes have the same muted, mustard-colored jackets: only the authors and titles vary. The books themselves stand out for their elegant design, thick paper, good printing, and comfortable heft in the hand. If you buy one Tartarus Book, it's safe to say you'll want to buy them all. And why not? As with Ash-Tree and Centipede titles, the books tend to go up in value, sometimes dramatically when they go out of print. Tartarus has recently been bringing out the complete works of Robert Aickman, the premier English author of "strange stories" of the past half-century (with Ramsey Campbell a close second). But they have also issued the major works of Arthur Machen, Lafcadio Hearn, Sarban, and Edith Wharton, among others. Tartarus, like the other presses, also publishes several outstanding contemporary masters of the eerie tale, including the incomparable Reggie Oliver, Mark Samuels, Rosalie Parker, Mark Valentine and Michael Reynier.

— Valancourt Books makes available in attractive paperback editions fairly rare books from the late 18th century to the present. Here one can find the gothic classics that frightened the heroines of Jane Austen's *Northanger Abbey,* the works of Bram Stoker other than *Dracula,* many of Richard Marsh's novels, starting with *The Beetle,* and some of the stranger weird or decadent literature of the 1890s. How can you possibly go wrong with Florence Marryat's 1897 *The Blood of the Vampire,* in which the heroine is the daughter of a mad scientist and a voodoo priestess?

The above are just a few of the more important small presses. But there are many others. This year Black Dog Books brought out *With the Hunted,* a magnificent collection of Sylvia Townsend Warner's scattered nonfiction. Sirius Fiction published *Gate of Horn, Book of Silk: A Guide to Gene Wolfe's 'The Book of the Long Sun' and 'The Book of the Short Sun,'* by Michael Andre-Driussi — and since Gene Wolfe is our greatest living writer of science fiction, and one of our greatest living writers period, this is an important study. Sundial Press has produced an exceptionally attractive edition of Phyllis Paul's *A Cage for the Nightingale,* likened to James's *The Turn of the Screw* in its power and artistry. One of our best writers of unsettling fiction, R. B. Russell, can be sampled in collections from Swan River Press (*Ghosts*) and PS Publishing (*Leave Your Sleep*). The stories of the writer-scholar Mark Valentine (some written with another fine fantasist, John Howard) can be enjoyed in collections from Swan River and Tartarus, while Exposition Internationale has produced an exquisite volume of his prose poems titled *At Dusk.*

While this week's "Browsings" column has gone on rather longer than I expected, all these publishers — and authors! — deserve your attention and support. I know my own life has been enriched by the work of these devoted bookmen and women.

P.S. Despite that obvious close, I just realized I hadn't mentioned my favorite small press publisher for kids: Bobbledy Books. Matthew Swanson writes the words, and his wife Robbi Behr creates the pictures, and together their books are silly, poetic, surreal, and incredibly cool. Their latest title is *Bobby and the Robots,* which ends by giving instructions on how to build a robot. Wise parents are advised to check out, then join the Bobbledy Books Club. Some readers may recall that Swanson and Behr, under their Idiots' Books imprint, produced that timeless, modern classic, *The Baby Is Disappointing.*

P.P.S. And how could I overlook Ramble House? Yes, its books are print-on-demands, but where else can you acquire the complete works of Harry Stephen Keeler, author of *The Man with the Magic Eardrums, The Skull of the Waltzing Clown,* and many, many others? Keeler is either the worst or the most original detective-story writer of all time. Ramble House is, in fact, pulp heaven, with reprints of Weird Tales authors and numerous oddities, such as Adams Farr's unique World War II novel, *The Fangs of Suet Pudding.* They certainly don't write 'em like that anymore.

Christmas Reading

Tis the season when choral societies start practicing their "Hallelujahs" and theaters around the country stage *A Christmas Carol.* Readers have their December traditions as well. To my mind there are two kinds of literate diversion particularly appropriate to the weeks just before and after Christmas: either Golden Age mysteries and ghost stories or what one might call "seasonal" poems and stories.

Into that first category falls the so-called "Christie for Christmas." For years, publishers brought out an Agatha Christie whodunit just in time for holiday gift-giving and, one assumes, post-holiday reading. But all sorts of genre writers have traded on the association of Christmas with cozy chills, Dickens being the pioneer and the story of Ebenezer Scrooge remaining the undisputed champeen.

Yet there are many other fine, lighthearted

Christmasy works, including the wonderful Dingley Dell chapters of Dickens's own *Pickwick Papers,* P. G. Wodehouse's "Jeeves and the Yule-tide Spirit," Damon Runyon's "The Three Wise Guys," and Jean Shepherd's "In God We Trust: All Others Pay Cash" (the basis for that nostalgia-rich and hilarious film *A Christmas Story*). To this day I am still moved by those two old-fashioned, sentimental classics, O. Henry's "The Gift of the Magi" and Henry Van Dyke's "The Story of the Other Wise Man."

Still, I'd like to recommend three of my particular favorites for the upcoming holidays — a novel, a poem, and a short story.

John Masefield's *The Box of Delights* begins a few days before Christmas as the English schoolboy Kay Harker is en route to visit his guardian and cousins near the cathedral town of Tatchester. On the train he meets a pair of sinister strangers, has his money stolen, and loses his ticket. When Kay finally reaches his station, he encounters an aged Punch-and-Judy puppeteer, who asks him to perform a small favor: "Master Harker, there is something that no other soul can do for me but you alone. As you go down toward Seekings, if you would stop at Bob's shop, as it were to buy muffins now. . . . Near the door you will see a woman plaided from the cold, wearing a ring of a very strange shape, Master Harker, being like my ring here, of the longways cross of gold and garnets. And she has bright eyes, Master Harker, as bright as mine, which is what few have. If you will step into Bob's shop to buy muffins now, saying nothing, not even to your good friend, and say to this Lady 'The Wolves are Running' then she will know and Others will know; and none will get bit."

Kay agrees and immediately afterward, in the distant fields, begins to glimpse what look like large Alsatian dogs "trying to catch a difficult scent." When the old Punch-and-Judy man next reappears, he gives Kay a small box for safekeeping. It is no ordinary box. I will say nothing further except that this terrific children's fantasy novel reaches its climax during Tatchester Cathedral's 1,000th Christmas Eve service.

Thomas Hardy's "The Oxen" — based on a legend that stable animals kneel on Christmas Eve — is short enough to quote here in its entirety. A "barton" is a farmyard, and a "coomb" is a hollow or valley:

"The Oxen"

Christmas Eve, and twelve of the clock.
"Now they are all on their knees,"
An elder said as we sat in a flock
By the embers in hearthside ease.
We pictured the meek mild creatures where
They dwelt in their strawy pen,
Nor did it occur to one of us there
To doubt they were kneeling then.
So fair a fancy few would weave
In these years! Yet, I feel,
If someone said on Christmas Eve,
"Come; see the oxen kneel,
In the lonely barton by yonder coomb
Our childhood used to know,"
I should go with him in the gloom,
Hoping it might be so.

This poem always brings a catch to my throat.

Arthur Conan Doyle's "The Blue Carbuncle" opens this way: "I had called upon my friend Sherlock Holmes upon the second morning after Christmas, with the intention of wishing him the compliments of the season." Before long, the great detective is dazzling poor old Watson with one of his most astonishing feats of deduction. A possible client has left behind his old hat:

"It is perhaps less suggestive than it might have been," he remarked, "and yet there are a few inferences which are very distinct, and a few others which represent at least a strong balance of probability. That the man was highly intellectual is of course obvious upon the face of it, and also that he was fairly well-to-do within the last three years, although he has now fallen upon evil days. He had foresight, but has less now than formerly, pointing to a moral retrogression, which, when taken with the decline of his fortunes, seems to indicate some evil influence, probably drink, at work upon him. This may account also for the obvious fact that his wife has ceased to love him."

With that, Holmes and Watson are off on the case of the stolen Christmas goose. Many Sherlockians reread this story every year, usually on December 27. It is, as Christopher Morley famously declared, "a Christmas story without slush," and one of the most charming of the adventures of the immortal duo of Baker Street.

Books for the Holidays

Giving books for the holidays is always a crapshoot. Sometimes the recipient will gush, "Oh, just what I always wanted — a deluxe pigskin-bound copy of Lydgate's *Fall of Princes.*" At other times, he or she will reply wanly, "Oh, a book. I just love books. I used to have some when I went to college." Most well-bred people are polite: "How thoughtful of you! One can never have too many novels by James Patterson." But others may blurt out: "Oh, darn! Another copy of *Fifty Shades of Grey*! What I was really hoping for was a cotton chenille housecoat and a pair of comfy wool socks. Or maybe a new toaster."

Given the general rate of failure and misfire, I've come to believe that one should simply give attractive copies of the books one loves. So here, arranged by age group, are some of my favorites (with a focus on literary and biographical/historical works).

I've listed just one or two titles by the chosen authors, but in most cases their other books are often just as good. I've also avoided classics that are either over-familiar or that seemed to lack an appropriately festive or fireside feel to them. So you won't find Ford Madox Ford's *The Good Soldier* ("This is the saddest story I have ever heard"), nor is there anything here by, say, Kafka, Faulkner, or Jean Rhys.

Bear in mind that the chronological ordering is, obviously, only approximate. Some people are more advanced readers than others, but good books for even the youngest kids are still enjoyable by the most mature grown-up. I would normally annotate such a list, but this would make for an inordinately long column, so I simply urge you to seek out some of these writers and their works in your local bookstore or online. A few titles may be out of print, but old copies are worth tracking down. Indeed, I'm firmly convinced that an old hardback — whether a first edition or not — is better than a recent paperback. But then I've never believed that a gift needed to be absolutely new, otherwise people wouldn't be buying antique earrings, let alone pre-owned BMWs, for their sweethearts.

Ages 1–4:

The Real Mother Goose, illustrated by Blanche Fisher Wright

We're Going on a Bear Hunt, by Michael Rosen; illustrated by Helen Oxenbury

The Random House Book of Poetry for Children, edited by Jack Prelutsky; illustrated by Arnold Lobel

Mike Mulligan and His Steam Shovel, by Virginia Lee Burton

The Travels of Babar, by Jean de Brunhoff

Ages 5–7:

Any good edition of the classic fairy tales

Bread and Jam for Frances, by Russell Hoban; illustrated by Lillian Hoban

A Day with Wilbur Robinson, by William Joyce

Jumanji, by Chris Van Allsburg

Miss Nelson is Missing! by Harry Allard; illustrated by James Marshall

Ages 8–11:

Alice's Adventures in Wonderland and *Alice Through the Looking Glass,* by Lewis Carroll; illustrated by John Tenniel

Five Children and It, by E. Nesbit

The Wind in the Willows, by Kenneth Grahame; illustrated by Ernest H. Shepard or Arthur Rackham

Homer Price, by Robert McCloskey

The Phantom Tollbooth, by Norton Juster; illustrated by Jules Feiffer

The Wolves of Willoughby Chase and *Blackhearts in Battersea,* by Joan Aiken

5 Novels: Alan Mendelsohn, the Boy from Mars; Slaves of Spiegel; The Last Guru; Young Adult Novel; The Snarkout Boys and the Avocado of Death, by Daniel Pinkwater

A Wrinkle in Time, by Madeleine L'Engle

The Hobbit, by J. R. R. Tolkien

The Sword in the Stone, by T. H. White

A Wizard of Earthsea, by Ursula K. Le Guin

Ages 11–15:

The Complete Sherlock Holmes, by A. Conan Doyle

Great Tales of Terror and the Supernatural, edited by Herbert Wise and Phyllis Fraser

Collected Ghost Stories, by M. R. James

101 Years' Entertainment: The Great Detective Stories, edited by Ellery Queen

The Science Fiction Hall of Fame, edited by Robert Silverberg (volume one: short stories; volumes two and three: novellas)

The Golden Argosy: A Collection of the Most Celebrated Short Stories in the English Language, edited by Van H. Cartmell and Charles Grayson

The White Nile and *The Blue Nile,* by Alan Moorehead

Endurance: Shackleton's Incredible Voyage, by Alfred Lansing

Ages 16–19:
She, by H. Rider Haggard
The Prisoner of Zenda, by Anthony Hope
The Grand Sophy, by Georgette Heyer
Lud-in-the-Mist, by Hope Mirrlees
The Lord of the Rings, by J. R. R. Tolkien
The Maltese Falcon, by Dashiell Hammett
The Thurber Carnival, by James Thurber
The Stars My Destination, by Alfred Bester
The Dying Earth, by Jack Vance
True Grit, by Charles Portis

Ages 19 and up:
Fiction:
Kim, by Rudyard Kipling
Seven Men, by Max Beerbohm
Leave it to Psmith, by P. G. Wodehouse
Crome Yellow, by Aldous Huxley
Gaudy Night, by Dorothy L. Sayers

The Master and Margarita, by Mikhail Bulgakov

The Leopard, by Giuseppe di Lampedusa

Gentlemen Prefer Blondes, by Anita Loos

The Moving Toyshop, by Edmund Crispin

The Locusts Have No King, by Dawn Powell

Pictures from an Institution, by Randall Jarrell

Nights at the Circus, by Angela Carter

A Fan's Notes, by Frederick Exley

Little Big Man, by Thomas Berger

Small World, by David Lodge

Amphigorey, by Edward Gorey

Nonfiction:

Poets of the English Language, edited by W. H. Auden and Norman Holmes Pearson (five volumes)

Individual editions of the poetry of T. S. Eliot, W. B. Yeats, Wallace Stevens, W. H. Auden, Philip Larkin, Elizabeth Bishop, and Anthony Hecht

Eothen, by Alexander Kinglake

Up in the Old Hotel, by Joseph Mitchell

The Best of Myles, by Flann O'Brien

Hindoo Holiday, by J. R. Ackerley

Dear Bunny, Dear Volodya: The Letters of Vladimir Nabokov and Edmund Wilson, edited by Simon Karlinsky

The Murder of Sir Edmund Godfrey, by
 John Dickson Carr
*The Letters of Nancy Mitford and Evelyn
 Waugh,* edited by Charlotte Mosley
*The Geography of the Imagination: Forty
 Essays,* by Guy Davenport
In Patagonia, by Bruce Chatwin
*The Habit of Being: Letters of Flannery
 O'Connor,* edited by Sally Fitzgerald
Midnight in the Garden of Good and Evil,
 by John Berendt
United States: Essays 1952–1992, by
 Gore Vidal

Well, I'd better stop. I'm beginning to
think of more and more titles. But remember: these are just some of the books that I
enjoy giving to people. Tastes may differ,
and I've no doubt overlooked the one work
that a) changed your life, b) to which you
return regularly for comfort and renewal, or
c) that you wished everyone in the world
knew about. At all events, I do think any of
the treasures listed above would make for
good reading on a cold winter's night (or
two or three). Happy holidays!

LET US NOW PRAISE
DOVER BOOKS

Last month my friend Tom Mann — author of *The Oxford Guide to Library Research* and, as Washington insiders know, the man to see at the reference desk of the Library of Congress — handed me a copy of a book entitled *Shakespeare, In Fact,* by Irvin Leigh Matus. Originally published in 1994 as a hardcover by Continuum, this carefully researched, data-rich, and beautifully written account of Shakespeare's life and career has now been reissued, quite handsomely, in paperback by Dover Books. I recommend it strongly, especially to Oxfordians, Baconians, and all the other groups who imagine that Shakespeare wasn't educated enough to write such brilliant plays.

Irv Matus, who died in 2011, by himself gives the lie to that elitist canard. As Tom points out in his introduction to this Dover edition, Irv "had no formal education beyond a high school diploma, but he wrote two of the best books ever on the Bard and his era. At the time he finished the first one, *Shakespeare: The Living Record,* 20 years ago, he was living on a heating grate behind the Library of Congress."

I won't say more about Tom's vivid portrait of Irv, except that it could have been printed by *The New Yorker* back when Joseph Mitchell, A. J. Liebling, and Wolcott Gibbs were writing profiles of gifted and eccentric characters. It almost goes without saying that Irv Matus was a proud member of Washington's most mysterious and exclusive association, facetiously referred to as The League of Extraordinary Gentlemen, but consisting of specialists and authorities on everything from forensic anthropology to fingerprints to South African politics and sociology. You can't apply to join the League, by the way, you can only be invited by its all-powerful president, a shadowy figure right out of Chesterton's *The Man Who Was Thursday.*

A few days after Tom gave me that new copy of *Shakespeare, In Fact,* I ran into Paul Dickson at a used bookstore. Paul — immensely genial, in both senses of the word — is himself an obvious candidate for the League. He's the biographer of legendary baseball owner Bill Veeck, an expert on language (*War Slang: American Fighting Words and Phrases Since the Civil War* is in its third edition), and a scout for Dover Books. In this last capacity, he keeps an eye out for old and odd works that should be returned to print. For instance, Paul introduced Dover's 2012 reissue of *Old-Time Camp Stoves and Fireplaces,* a practical manual first published in 1937 by the Civilian Conservation Corps. (My father might have used the original, since he joined the CCC in his youth and worked in some out-of-the-way parts of California.) Paul also wrote the text for *Courage in the Moment: The Civil Rights Struggle, 1961–1964,* a recent Dover "original" built around Jim Wallace's you-are-there photographs of protests and sit-ins. Not least, this astonishingly energetic and prolific author helped Tom engineer the re-publication of *Shakespeare, In Fact.*

On my way home from chatting with Paul, I started to think about Dover Books and their importance in my own reading life. Because of Dover paperbacks, I was introduced to M. R. James's *Ghost Stories of an Antiquary* and to the adventures of Ernest Bramah's blind detective Max Carrados, marveled at the great cases of Jacques Futrelle's Professor S. F. X. Van Dusen, known as The Thinking Machine, and was awed by the cosmic science fiction of Olaf Stapledon's *Last and First Men* and *Star Maker.* Because of Dover Books I was gradually able to accumulate a small library of wonderful and unusual titles, ranging from the mysteries and ghost stories of Sheridan Le Fanu, to H. P. Lovecraft's groundbreaking essay, *Supernatural Horror in Literature,* to Martin Gardner's first great debunking classic, *Fads and Fallacies in the Name of Science.*

In those days of yore, Dover proudly trumpeted that their paperbacks were "designed for years of use," that the paper wouldn't deteriorate, and that the pages consisted of sewn signatures, with ample margins. Sometimes the outer cellophane layer of the covers would delaminate, but this didn't affect the book in any serious manner: It would still open flat, and the type face, except in those publications that reproduced the actual pages of old magazine serials, would always be large and legible. In short, a Dover book was "a permanent book." Best of all, the company's offerings were cheap — only a few dollars new and often findable for even less in thrift shops and second-hand bookstores. There must still be a couple of dozen Dover editions scattered around this house. Even now I sometimes take one out and study the lists of "titles of related interest" printed on either the inside covers or as an appendix.

For example, at the back of *Three Martian Novels* by Edgar Rice Burroughs, there are 15 pages describing books about science, philosophy, history, and languages. You could buy W. P. Ker's enthralling *Epic and Romance,* or E. K. Rand's *Founders of the Middle Ages,* or W. G. Sumner's *Folkways.* In my copy of *Best Ghost Stories of Algernon Blackwood,* the inside cover carries an extensive list of "Dover Mystery, Detective, Ghost Stories, and Other Fiction," including Lafcadio Hearn's *Kwaidan,* G. K. Chesterton's *The Man Who Was Thursday,* and *Five Victorian Ghost Novels,* edited by E. F. Bleiler.

Everett F. Bleiler! Even as a boy, I noticed that this Bleiler guy introduced many of the books I most cared about. He seemed to have read everything, and, as I later learned, he actually had. To this day, I keep *The Guide to Supernatural Fiction* and Ev's two similar volumes about early science fiction near my bed for late-night browsing: They are among the world's most beloved, and valuable, reference books. In the first, Bleiler lists and annotates — i.e., summarizes, with capsule judgments — 1,775 books from 1750 to 1960, "including short stories, weird fiction, stories of supernatural horror, fantasy, Gothic novels, occult fiction, and similar literature." Because many, if not most, of those 1,775 titles are collections or anthologies, that means Bleiler read literally thousands of pieces of great, good, and wholly ephemeral genre literature. The science fiction volumes cover many additional thousands of novels and stories.

These splendid books — perhaps the greatest publications ever of Kent State University Press, yet now sadly out of print — are the harvest of a lifetime of reading. For more than 20 years Bleiler worked as an editor, later an executive vice president, at Dover, and was responsible for rediscovering and making available some of the most important titles in Victorian and Edwardian popular fiction. He was himself an exceptionally learned man, having written a Japanese grammar, produced a scholarly edition of Nostradamus, and contributed regularly to specialized journals about arcane works of Renaissance allegory and fantasy.

He was also kindly, generous, and modest, and I am proud to have exchanged letters and phone calls with him, and once — only once, alas — to have met him for a bookish lunch in New York. He is one of the heroes of modern literary scholarship, and I wish I'd gotten to know him more and better.

But his legacy remains. Many — and it really should be all — of his Dover editions remain in print. His great reference volumes are standard bibliographic tools for antiquarian bookdealers: "Not in Bleiler" is the sign of a truly rare work. His son Richard Bleiler, moreover, continues to extend his father's scholarship, and has added his own researches to it.

Sigh. What I wouldn't give to be 14 years old again, on Christmas break from school, and reading, for the first time, *Gods, Men, and Ghosts,* Bleiler's selection from Lord Dunsany's gorgeously written and clever fantasies. Oh, well. There's one thing the adult me knows for sure: If Ev were alive today and living in Washington, and if he could be persuaded to join, he would certainly be one of the most extraordinary members of The League of Extraordinary Gentlemen.

A Dreamer's Tale

For those of us with an inward turn of mind, which is another name for melancholy introspection, the beginning of a new year inevitably leads to thoughts about both the future and the past. My father would often intone on significant birthdays or anniversaries: "That which I did I ought not to have done, that which I did not do I ought to have done." His pseudo-biblical lament unfortunately reduces the past to one long series of regrets, to the memory of foolish choices or rosy daydreams about what might have been.

That way, I suspect, madness lies. Also, the ire of one's spouse and children — What about us? they might rightly complain. Are we chopped liver or something? After all, people do make good choices, often very good ones. But in recollection we inevitably tend to think about those mysterious and alluring roads not taken. Could I have become a novelist or a poet? Did I miss my true destiny by not moving to New York or San Francisco? Might I have been happier as a small-town librarian or a plumber? Did I use my small talents in the best possible way?

Such dreamy speculations are, happily, of no real consequence. They make us thoughtful for a moment; then we sigh and get on with the day's work. To those who do what lies within them, according to nominalist theology, God will not deny grace.

Like most people, at the beginning of a new year, I get revved up about what I want to accomplish in the coming 12 months. In 2013 I resolve to go to the gym every other day. I will lose 15 pounds and get back into what a friend used to call, when she was looking for a fresh boyfriend, "fighting trim." I will write a short story and start a new book. I will travel more and see the world. I will fix up this dilapidated house, or sell it, and make a proper library for myself. I will . . . I resolve to . . . I must. . . .

Some of these high-minded resolutions will almost certainly come to pass. [Note from 2015: With the possible exception of a short trip to England, I failed to accomplish any of them.] But what I really want to do, if I were to follow my bliss, as Joseph

Campbell used to counsel us, is simultaneously modest and fanciful: to travel around North America in a van visiting second-hand bookstores. During my travels I'd also make occasional detours to spend a day or two with old friends, now too little seen — with my high school buddies who live in Houston and Missouri, my college chums in Maine and Chicago, my former book-collecting partner David Streitfeld, ensconced in the Bay Area, even some folks up in Toronto and British Columbia.

Being a hero (and heroine) worshipper, I'd naturally take the time to genuflect at the final resting places of writers I admire. (Even now, two of my favorite photographs depict a reverent me at the tomb of Stendhal in Paris and the grave of Eudora Welty in Jackson, Mississippi.) Come lunchtime I would obviously eat in diners and always order pie for dessert, sometimes à la mode. During the evenings, sipping a local beer in some one-night cheap motel, I would examine the purchases of the day and fall asleep reading shabby, half-forgotten novels.

Why would anyone want to do this? Mainly for the adventure, to recapture a little of the swagger and almost inexpressible sense of freedom that belong only to youth. It's certainly not as though I need any more books. Just yesterday I was up in the attic creating neat stacks of those I would like to read Right Now. While admiring one such book tower, I suddenly flashed on the famous *Twilight Zone* episode, "Time Enough at Last," in which Burgess Meredith, amid the ruins of a post-nuclear holocaust world, makes his own To Be Read pile — and then stumbles, breaking his glasses.

What books would I read if I could simply read for my own sweet pleasure? Well, there are at least a dozen major classics of English fiction that I've never quite gotten round to yet. Samuel Richardson's *Clarissa,* for example, and — hangs head in shame — Henry James's *Portrait of a Lady.* There are, alas, others comparably important. But, in truth, the books I most want to read are far stranger than these approved canonical high spots. What titles, you ask?

First, two books by Cutcliffe Hyne: *The Lost Continent,* a classic novel about Atlantis, and *The Adventures of Captain Kettle,* tales of the criminous and fantastical that once rivaled those of Sherlock Holmes in popularity, just as Richard Marsh's *The Beetle* — another book I look forward to — outsold Bram Stoker's *Dracula.* Then there's the autobiographical *Paul Kelver,* by Jerome K. Jerome (author of the comic masterpiece, *Three Men in a Boat*), and Maurice Baring's *Daphne Adeane,* about a strange portrait and the interconnection of ghosts and living people, and Robert Ames Bennet's *Thyra: A Romance of the Polar Pit,* in which explorers encounter a Viking-like civilization living within the hollow earth, and Russell Thorndike's *The Slype,* a hard-to-find mystery by the creator of Dr. Syn, aka The Scarecrow of Romney Marsh. [Note from 2015: I've since enjoyed nearly all these books.]

I've read, and written about, Claude Houghton's existential thriller *I Am Jonathan Scrivener,* but I'd like to look into his other novels, especially those with male names in the titles: *This Was Ivor Trent, Julian Grant Loses His Way, Hudson Rejoins the Herd.* Similarly, I've long meant to read more T. S. Stribling, not just his mystery stories about Dr. Poggioli, such as *Clues of the Caribbees,* but also his satirical novels, especially his semi-fantasy about academia, *These Bars of Flesh.* I've also got copies of several minor classics of supernatural fiction just waiting for their moment: Alexander Laing's *The Cadaver of Gideon Wyck,* Hans Heinz Ewers's *Alraune,* Frances Young's *Cold Harbor,* and Leonard Cline's

The Dark Chamber (a favorite of H. P. Love-craft).

Then, too, I've been saving for the right holiday or vacation such oddball whodunits as Caryl Brahms and S. J. Simon's comic *A Bullet in the Ballet* and T. E. B. Clarke's alternate history *Murder at Buckingham Palace* and Michael Fessier's mix of fantasy, Grand Guignol, and mystery, *Fully Dressed and in His Right Mind.* Isn't that an irresist-ible title? Given time, I'd certainly sample more of the work of Clemence Dane, start-ing with *The Moon Is Feminine,* and explore that of Phyllis Paul, beginning with the recently reissued *A Cage for the Nightingale.* And then there's J. A. Mitchell's *The Last American,* subtitled "A Fragment from the Journal of Khan-Li, Prince of Dimph-Yoo-Chur and Admiral in the Persian Navy." It was written in 1889.

Not least are all the works I long to read but that are essentially unprocurable (in hardcover at least), except through interli-brary loan or to those who can afford to pay more than $500 for a single book. Frank Walford's *Twisted Clay,* written in the 1930s, set in Australia, and immediately banned, is about a lesbian serial killer. Murray Con-stantine's *Swastika Night,* published in

1937, envisions a horrific Nazi-controlled world, 500 years in the future. Then there's R. C. Ashby's *He Arrived at Dusk* and Eugene Lee Hamilton's *The Lord of the Dark Red Star* and Mortimer Collins's 1874 occult novel, *Transmigration* (which includes a section set on Mars), and Oliver Onions's *The Hand of Kornelius Voyt* (by the author of the famous ghost story "The Beckoning Fair One") and Frederick Irving Anderson's two volumes about master criminals, *The Adventures of the Infallible Godahl* and *The Notorious Sophie Lang.* And many more. [Another note from 2015: Some of these have now been reprinted by specialty presses.]

Given such alluring titles on my bookshelves or precariously arranged in stacks up in the attic, I really do need a long life, with good vision and intact mental faculties. Hope springs eternal! Of course, the id side of my reader's brain tells me that I really should reread *War and Peace* and *The Magic Mountain,* or start on *The Portrait of a Lady,* rather than pick up that copy of *The Messiah of the Cylinder,* by Victor Rousseau, or *Dr. Nikola's Vendetta,* by Guy Boothby. Sigh, truth is, I really do enjoy big, serious, life-changing *Great Books of the Western*

World–style classics. But I also like weird, old stuff.

With the possible exception of steampunk aficionados, many reasonable people must view my fascination with Victorian and Edwardian popular fiction — mysteries, fantasy, and adventure — as eccentric or merely antiquarian. Still, these books, despite some period prejudices, do offer good storytelling, moral clarity, and an escape from our meretricious times. Best of all, for me they also deliver something of the cozy pleasure I got when, as a boy, I first opened *The Hound of the Baskervilles,* or followed Tarzan into the forbidden city of Opar, or tagged along on Jules Verne's *Journey to the Center of the Earth.* Besides, I'm also an invested member of The Baker Street Irregulars, which meets in a few days for its annual get-together in New York. To a serious Irregular it is always 1895 — or at least it is for one long weekend in early January.

MONEY

While reading the papers this past Monday, I paused over two stories. One was a *Washington Post* review by Patrick Anderson — who specializes in writing about crime fiction — of a new thriller by Dick Wolf called *The Intercept.* In his opening paragraph Anderson mentioned all the millions Wolf had made from his TV shows, *Law & Order* in particular, and ended by observing that the writer owned a home in Montecito, California, "which is, as the saying goes, where God would live if he had the money."

The second story I lingered over was in *The Wall Street Journal.* According to reporter Jennifer Smith, prominent law firms are now letting go partners who don't bring in enough business or bill enough hours. As one unidentified source said, quite plainly, "It isn't enough to be a good lawyer. The job is to make money for the firm."

Apparently, these are tough times for that

most universally despised of all professions. Some years back, and perhaps still, the Folger Shakespeare Library sold T-shirts emblazoned with the words: "The first thing we do, let's kill all the lawyers." (That's from *Henry VI, Part Two,* if you want to look it up.) Of course, nowadays lawyers enjoy lots of competition when it comes to being reviled. Consider, for instance, Wall Street bankers, hedge-fund operators, and over-paid CEOs (i.e., virtually all of them). Many of these are, of course, lawyers as well.

Like most people, I am troubled by salary inequities. Long ago, when I took "Introduction to Economics," my teacher, Robert Tufts, scribbled on one of my term papers (which had vigorously defended the radical views of Henry George's *Progress and Poverty*), "Mr. Dirda, you actually write pretty well, but you don't understand economics at all." Perhaps so.

Basically, I think that most people either make too much money or not enough money. The jobs that are essential and important pay too little, and those that are essentially managerial pay far too much. In a reasonable society, for instance, all elementary education would be public education and the highest-paid profession would logically be that of schoolteacher. The men

and women to whom we entrust the forma-
tion of our children's minds and characters
would be deeply honored and appropriately
rewarded. That teachers are not is largely
because the rich send their kids to private
schools. These should be prohibited. At that
point, our politicians — one of the overpaid
groups, in my view — would quickly ensure
that public schools employed the best and
brightest people that money could buy.

But when was the last time you heard
middle-class parents express the hope that
their most gifted child, the one with the
double 800s on his or her SATs, would find
a job as a third-grade teacher? And why
don't parents wish this, rather than hope
that little Chauncey or Rasheeda will grow
up to become a corporate attorney or
cardiac surgeon? Because of money and
status. We still measure success by the Mer-
cedes in the driveway and the size of the
McMansion.

The goal of a just society should be to
provide satisfying work, with a living wage,
to all its citizens. The jobs that are vitally
important, truly dangerous or stressful, or
inherently unattractive, should be the best
compensated: teachers, coal-miners,
emergency-room nurses, physicians and
PAs, hospice workers, and, yes, trash collec-

tors should all be extremely well paid. But work that deals mainly with intangibles, with the manipulation of words or numbers, should largely be its own reward. Corporate executives, who love to wheel and deal, ought to earn no more than poets, who love to play with language. In fact, I think that everyone employed by a business, whether a guy on the assembly line, a secretary, or the chief financial officer, should make exactly the same amount. Each does what he or she can do best for the success of the product or the company. A job should bring enough for a worker and family to live on, but after that, self-realization, the exercise of one's gifts and talents, is what truly matters.

Tolstoy once asked, How much land does a man need? The answer, you may recall, measured six feet by three: the size of a cemetery plot. How much money does a 21st-century American need? Not millions a year, not the kind of salaries we bestow on many in what is loosely called "business." The rich soon come to think that they deserve to take home grotesque sums annually, that they are, in essence, being reasonably compensated, and that any attempt to tax them a tiny bit more is unjust and undemocratic. Yet why is this? A life is a life. Self-fulfillment, the expansive exercise of one's abilities, should be, and usually is, what matters to most of us. The only reward that counts, in the end, is to be honored for one's accomplishments, whether by colleagues, employees, or the nation.

No doubt such thinking will be dubbed, or denounced, as socialistic or un-American. It's certainly completely Utopian. But I am a child of both the working class and the 1960s. I don't like gross monetary favoritism. I firmly believe that the wrong people and the wrong professions are being rewarded, and rewarded absurdly, and that the hardest work the obscenely rich do is ensuring that they preserve their privileges, status symbols, and bloated bank accounts. Of course, no one ever listens to me. But after the deplorable behavior of our legislative officials in dealing with the latest fiscal crisis, after the childish, know-nothing recalcitrance of the Tea Party, after the almost weekly corruption scandals among our moguls and financial "advisors," after the outrageous golden parachutes allocated to inept executives, and, most of all, after the general and ongoing contempt demonstrated by the haves for the have-nots, it's enough to make even a mild-mannered book reviewer depressed and ashamed of his country.

Book Projects

Last week I made my annual pilgrimage to New York for the 2013 birthday weekend of The Baker Street Irregulars. The BSI, as many of this column's readers probably know, is the 80-year-old literary and dining society devoted to honoring Sherlock Holmes and Dr. Watson. Yes, a few people do dress up in Victorian garb or sport deerstalkers, but mainly the BSI meets for talks, presentations, and what churches call "fellowship." In effect, this means three days of eating and drinking, followed by more drinking.

There is, technically speaking, a good deal of planned programming. I attended the Lunch of Steele — honoring Sherlockian illustrator Frederic Dorr Steele — held at The Players in Gramercy Park, a bibulous Special Meeting at The Coffee House Club (of which BSI founder Christopher Morley was a member), the Gillette Lunch at

Moran's Seafood Restaurant (a double homage, as William Gillette played the Great Detective on stage for 40 years and the name Moran recalls that of Professor Moriarty's chief assassin, Colonel Sebastian Moran), the black-tie BSI banquet at the Yale Club, a late-night champagne party hosted by Otto Penzler of The Mysterious Bookshop, a private cocktail party on Central Park West on Saturday afternoon, and, finally, a gathering of the Pondicherry Lodgers for Indian food later that same evening, succeeded by nightcaps even later before the fireplace at the Harvard Club.

Of course, those with real stamina could also attend several additional lunches, dinners, and alcoholic get-togethers. But, alas, I'm not the man I once was. During the few hours my dance card wasn't penciled in, I sped woozily away — via subway — to visit the Strand Bookstore, the Housing Works Bookstore, James Cummins Bookseller, and The Grolier Club. I naturally acquired a few items in the Sherlockian dealers' room as well, including two T-shirts, Robert Veld's immensely informative *The Strand Magazine and Sherlock Holmes,* Nicholas Utechin's diverting *"Occasionally to Embellish": Some Writings on Sherlock Holmes,* and the latest magisterial production of the BSI itself: *The*

Wrong Passage: A Facsimile of the Original Manuscript of "The Golden Pince-Nez," with Annotations and Commentary, edited by Robert Katz and Andrew Solberg. Needless to say, it was a heavy suitcase that your "Browsings" columnist rolled down 6th Avenue when he boarded the nine A.M. Bolt Bus for the trip back to Washington.

While the BSI blowout is always fun, especially for those who have trained for it or possess, by genetic gift, the capacity for drink of 1930s newspapermen, I was constantly being asked a question that bothered me. It's one that any writer, journalist, or scholar will recognize: "What are you working on now?" This actually means: What is your latest book project?

While I explained, with the becoming modesty for which I am widely celebrated, that I was writing every day and contributing regularly to a half dozen newspapers and periodicals, such journalism, no matter how exigent or ambitious, doesn't really seem to count. People want to know about books. *On Conan Doyle* came out in 2011, and it's now 2013 — shouldn't I be finishing up something new?

Well, yes, I should. Or at least starting on it. But what?

I've never found it easy to come up with

publishing projects. Three of my books —
Readings, Bound to Please, and *Classics for
Pleasure* — are essentially collections of my
columns and reviews. In some instances,
the pieces have been amplified or reworked
so that they read like essays. *An Open Book*
is a memoir, focused on how comics, adventure stories, and classics shaped my early
life. *Book by Book* is a little compendium of
quotations drawn from my commonplace
book, i.e., from the bound volume into
which I've been copying favorite passages
from my reading for the past 40 years; B3
— as I sometimes call it — is organized by
subject and supplemented by mini-essays
and book lists. *On Conan Doyle* chronicles,
from an autobiographical viewpoint, my
lifelong involvement with the novels, stories,
essays, and memoirs of A. Conan Doyle,
starting with my discovery, in 5th grade, of
The Hound of the Baskervilles. It's only 200
pages long, part of a Princeton series called
"Writers on Writing."

Obviously all these titles fall, more or less,
into the category of "books about books."
Stories and poems and works of history and
humane letters are all I ever write about,
albeit through a very personal lens whenever
possible. As I've said more than once, I shy
away from calling myself a critic — I don't

possess that kind of analytic mind, though I also hope that I'm more entertaining than most of the critics I read. (Sorry, no names.) In fact, I'm a bookman, an appreciator, a cheerleader for the old, the neglected, the marginalized, and the forgotten. On sunny days I may call myself a literary journalist.

What I enjoy about reviewing and writing for newspapers and periodicals is simply the chance to talk about all kinds of books and lots of them. Last week, for *The Washington Post,* I reviewed a reissue of Shepherd Mead's humorous *How to Live Like a Lord Without Really Trying;* this week, I'm indulging a lifelong fascination with religion by writing about *Trent: What Happened at the Council,* and the week following that I'll be discussing the noir fiction of Cornell Woolrich. *Harper's Magazine* recently ran my overview of Thornton Wilder's varied and undervalued work, while *The Weekly Standard* published my reflections on the nonfiction of A. J. A. Symons (author of the biographical classic, *The Quest for Corvo*) and *Bookforum* brought out a piece about George Minois's *The Atheist's Bible,* a historical study of a late medieval polemic attacking "the three impostors" Moses, Christ, and Mohammed. In the next couple of months I'll be taking on subjects as various as John Keats, the fantasies of M. P. Shiel, the short stories of Sherwood Anderson, some recent science fiction scholarship, and the fiction of James Salter, among much else, including those inexorable weekly reviews for *The Post*. Close friends, or those in my pay, sometimes call me a literary polymath, while others say that I'm just a shallow dilettante, superficial and breezy, with a faux-naif style. You be the judge (and for those who'd like to be in my pay — please send in your application).

Of course, all this work is merely journalism, and it's hard to make it seem anywhere near as important as a book. Indeed, it isn't. Books possess a shape and permanence that scattered pieces — *disjecta membra* — don't.

When I talk to friends and editors about possible projects, especially about projects that might come with a significant cash advance, they usually suggest a biography. Sometimes I'm tempted, but the prospect of spending years researching and writing about someone else's life offends my vanity. I don't want to submerge myself in another man or woman's existence, I want to write about *me,* about the books and writers that *I* like. And I want to be able to finish any commitment within a year at best, so that I can get on to something else. I have, it would seem, the temperament of a reporter — always intensely interested in a subject for a week, but soon ready to move on to the next assignment.

For a while now I did have one big project in mind: "The Great Age of Storytelling." I hoped to write about the amazing flowering of popular fiction in England and elsewhere from roughly 1860 to 1930. All the modern genres really start then, and during this period many of our iconic figures sprang to life, from Peter Pan to The Scarlet Pimpernel. Alas, back in 2010, when I first suggested such a book, no trade publisher was willing to fork out enough cash to support my household for two years, the time I felt I needed to do a good job. I may try again in the near future, perhaps approaching a university press, but I would still require a significant amount of money. That's something in short supply at universities these days.

Of course, what I really *should* do is turn my energies to creating a reality TV show called *Books*. While I was in New York, I managed a couple of quick coffees with my son Mike, who works for a big public relations firm there. He told me that his classmate from Oberlin College, a young woman named Lena Dunham, was voted the coolest person in America by *Time* magazine. She is, I've since learned, the driving force behind an award-winning television series called *Girls.* I've never seen it. It would be kind of creepy if I had. Still, I just read that the fortunate Ms. Dunham has received a $3.5 million book contract. I suppose that whatever she writes will attract one or two more readers than something called "The Great Age of Storytelling."

Sigh. Cutting edge I'll never be, unless, of course, old-fashioned suddenly becomes hip and cool. Which could happen, right? Right?

[Note: I eventually found a publisher for *The Great Age of Storytelling,* though the advance was modest. I'm hoping the book will appear in 2016.]

ENDING UP

Over the past year I've enjoyed writing these "Browsings" essays, meditations, and rants. The time has quite sped by. I hope you — whoever you are — have enjoyed reading them. Some of them anyway.

At all events, last week I decided it was time to pass this particular baton to someone else. *The American Scholar*'s editors have not yet announced my successor, but fairly soon you will discover a new name gracing the Friday slot on the magazine's website. I hope you'll give that new person a try.

While I'll probably contribute columns for another week or two, I thought it worthwhile to try and settle in my own mind why I am walking away from work that I enjoy. Time is one reason. I find, to recall a favorite saying of my father, that every 15-minute job now ends up taking an hour. Another is coming up with new topics. I envy those bloggers who can express strong opinions about everything. Me, I just metaphorically saunter along, whistling a happy tune, and hope that my effusions turn out to be mildly entertaining.

More and more, though, I worry that my pen has gleaned my teeming brain and that what I produce is weary, stale, flat, and unprofitable. (Guess the sources of the two quotations — both mentioned and identified in earlier columns — and win a prize!) The furrows of the brain occasionally need to lie fallow.

And still another reason is money. I do live by my pen, or keyboard, and while there's considerable prestige attached to writing for the *Scholar,* it doesn't reward its contributors as handsomely as, say, *The New Yorker* or *Esquire* — not that I've ever written for either of those magazines. *The American Scholar* is an intellectual quarterly and what it lacks in lavish compensation, it makes up for in intelligent, appreciative readers.

Still, I have developed some low-grade champagne tastes, especially in my book collecting, which all by itself demands a healthy bank balance. In my youth, I was happy just to unearth any copy of, say, E. F. Benson's mystery *The Blotting Book.* I now own both the English and the American first editions. These aren't terribly pricey items, to be sure — one cost $35 and the other $15 — but if you buy lots of such treasures, it gradually adds up.

For instance, just this past Wednesday I tore myself away from this desk and drove downtown to have lunch with the poet and translator A. M. Juster. Juster is the pen name of a very senior government official who translates Latin poetry, often fairly obscure Latin poetry, as a pastime. Sounds positively Victorian, doesn't it? And wholly admirable too. Gladstone, England's most famous 19th-century prime minister, built a personal library of more than 32,000 volumes and it was for use, not ostentation. His rival Disraeli, when out of power, brought out excellent and witty novels. At best our leading politicians may occasionally open a book if shown how. Former presidential hopeful Newt Gingrich did crank out some pot-boiling adventure fiction, but that's not quite the same thing.

After an extremely enjoyable lunch (Juster had onion soup, I had moussaka), with talk — and I'm not kidding about this — of Maximianus's elegies, acrostic poetry, and the riddles of Aldhelm, I said goodbye and hurried back to my car with three minutes to spare on the parking meter. At that point I should have pointed my wife's Prius toward Silver Spring and gone home.

Needless to say, I didn't.

Instead I drove toward Second Story Books in Dupont Circle and spent 15 minutes looking for a place to park. I then scouted the offerings ($3 each) on the bookstore's sidewalk shelves and turned up a nice first of *The Panic Hand,* a collection of Jonathan Carroll's elegant and eerie short stories. Long ago, when I reviewed one of his early novels — *Sleeping in Flame* — I described its overall feel as a cross between the magazines *Weird Tales* and *Vanity Fair.*

At which point, I really should have plunked down my $3, taken my purchase, and gone home.

Needless to say, I didn't.

Instead I sauntered into the store itself and began, just idly, to look around. Right away I noticed a copy of Baron Corvo's *Hubert's Arthur* for $100, but decided that was too much, especially since I'd just recently written about Corvo and his biographer A. J. A. Symons for *The Weekly Standard.* I wasn't likely to read any more of this paranoid decadent's work for a while. So I poked around some more. I nearly bought a very nice first of M. F. K. Fisher's

Map of Another Town, her account of a long sojourn in Aix-en-Provence. I'm fond of this book because I too once lived in Aix, and, as it happened, roomed for six weeks with the same landlady as Fisher. But I knew Madame Wytenhove 20 years later. I sometimes fantasize that the gorgeous Mary Frances and I slept in the same bed.

But I already owned *Map of Another Town,* so even though it was just $6, I left it on the shelf for some other lucky Francophile.

I kept on browsing. I thought about a somewhat worn copy of Mark Girouard's *The Victorian Country House,* but I've got a stack of his books on the piano now, including *Life in the English Country House* and *The Return to Camelot.* I figured I should wait and see if I read those two before I began buying more Girouard. Sound logic, yes, but I now rather regret leaving the book.

After exploring the fiction, art and architecture, literary criticism, and poetry sections, I lingered over science fiction and fantasy. The store was selling paperbacks of William Morris's prose romances, in the Ballantine Adult Fantasy series edited by Lin Carter, for $4 apiece. The thing is, I own some of the Morris books already — I knew I had *The Well at the World's End* because it bears one of the most haunting titles in all of English literature. But did *The Sundering Flood* and *The Wood Beyond the World* repose somewhere in a box in the basement? I thought so but couldn't remember. In the end, I placed the Second Story copies back on the shelf.

As usual, I then wandered through mythology and folklore — nothing — followed by history. In the Medieval section I pulled out a first edition of Andreas Capellanus's *The Art of Courtly Love,* translated by John Jay Parry and published by Columbia in 1941. I'd studied a paperback of this 12th-century rule-book for lovers back in college, and then a revised version in graduate school. But I don't really like paperbacks — except for 1950s mysteries with sleazy covers featuring blondes in dishabille — and this was a handsome, if jacketless, hardback, and I just wanted it. So, I shelled out $15 and finally prepared to go home.

But I didn't.

On the way out a bookcase full of elegant sets, some leather-bound, caught my eye. Now I admit to mixed feelings about *Oeuvres Completes* and long rows of matching books — altogether too official-looking — but I noticed that there were seven or eight Pléiade editions displayed, including the two volumes of Flaubert's collected novels. As

God is my witness, to quote the immortal Scarlett O'Hara, I opened one of them and my eyes fell on my favorite passage from *The Temptation of St. Anthony,* the section where the Queen of Sheba appears to the austere anchorite to tempt him with the delights of her body. Her enticements rise to a climax with the words: "Je ne suis pas une femme, je suis un monde." And it was just those words I had opened to: "I am not a woman, I am a world."

So, naturally I had to buy the Flauberts, since one doesn't just casually defy the *Sortes Virgilianae:* The book gods would withdraw their favor. Still, I like Pléiades and own quite a few. Okay, more than a few. As everyone says, they really are more attractive than the slightly clunky Library of America titles and these two were bargain-priced. In a twinkling, the Dirda bank balance was down another $40.

At which point, I really, really should have gotten in my car and driven home.

But did I? Need you ask?

Instead I headed down P Street to Georgetown and The Lantern Bookshop, operated for the benefit of Bryn Mawr College. There I wandered in and noticed, on the rare and vintage shelf, a copy of Robert Byron's *The Road to Oxiana,* the 1930s travel classic about the Middle East and Central Asia. I already possessed the Oxford paperback of this book and the handsome Folio Society hardback of it, too. But this John Lehmann edition called to me — it had been published in 1950 and it would match my John Lehmann edition of Byron's *The Station* (about Mount Athos). It wasn't the first edition, which appeared in 1937, so I discussed the price with the manager and it was dropped to $25.

That wouldn't have been so bad, except that I'd also spotted a copy of Italo Calvino's *The Castle of Crossed Destinies* for the same price — as well as nice $5 editions of Angus Wilson's first novel, *Hemlock and After,* and Barbara Pym's *Quartet in Autumn,* the latter the English first. Plus there was this book called *Twenty Years in Paris,* by some guy named Robert Sherard I'd never heard of, but that featured photographs of 19th-century literary eminences, including a striking one of Maupassant. At $5 I had to get that too. I later looked Sherard's book up online and discovered it was, in theory, worth quite a bit more than I'd paid for it. Always gratifying. Often it turns out the other way round.

In the end I dropped $75 at The Lantern. And at that point I finally did go home, where I surreptitiously smuggled my new acquisitions into the house.

Now this is bad, very bad. These days I can hardly step away from this desk and not find myself gravitating to a used-book store and pulling out my credit card. I can almost always justify my purchases as sensible, reasonable courses of action. All addicts do this. Still, those book outlays add up quite dramatically when the monthly Visa bill comes due.

So that's why I'm bringing the "Browsings" column to a close. I've got to figure out how to break into *Vanity Fair* or *The New Yorker,* where the big bucks are. Bloody likely. But it's either that or take a part-time job at Second Story Books or the Friends of the Library Book Sale Room in Wheaton. Those employee discounts would come in mighty handy.

A POSITIVELY, FINAL
APPEARANCE

As it happens, this will be — to borrow the title of the third installment of Alec Guinness's autobiography — my "positively, final appearance," at least as the Friday "Browsings" columnist. No doubt the *Scholar*'s persuasive editors will occasionally inveigle me into writing a book review or article for the print magazine. In the meantime, thank you all for reading my effusions of the past year.

By this point anything else I say is bound to sound anticlimactic, and I should probably just take a bow, wave cheerio, and exit stage left. But I do have a few last thoughts to share. Let me number them, as it conveys the impression that I've thought systematically about all these matters.

1) my mind, reading should be a pleasure and, through these columns, I've tried to pass along some of the excitement and

rewards of my own bookish life. All too often the work of today's literary journalists calls to mind a remark made by Wilfred Sheed about the once-well-known critic Irving Howe. What Sheed said, more or less, was this: When you read Irving Howe's criticism, you can tell that he's not doing it for fun.

I certainly hope these various essays, in their differing, dithering ways, have been fun. I've done my best to be amusing, silly, and sometimes a little weird. As my old friend Bill Greider, the national affairs correspondent for *The Nation,* once told me: Writing that isn't fun to read usually doesn't get read.

2) hope that the past 50 or so columns have reminded readers that the world of books is bigger than the current best-seller list. Thirty-five years ago this spring, I was hired as an assistant editor at *The Washington Book World.* Before long, I quietly inaugurated my own personal crusade: to entice people to try unexpected books, old books, neglected books, genre books, upsetting books, downright strange books. May I share a favorite, and famous, passage from Kafka? "The books we need are the kind that act upon us like a misfortune, that

make us suffer like the death of someone we love more than ourselves, that make us feel as though we were on the verge of suicide, or lost in a forest remote from all human habitation — a book should serve as the ax for the frozen sea within us."

Once, this seemed to me to describe the sort of soul-shattering literary experiences we should always be seeking. Not so much now. For Kafka, reading, like criticism of the Irving Howe school, was something you didn't just do for fun. It was hard work and you needed to use an ax and you probably felt exhausted afterwards and ready for some hot compresses.

There are, of course, books — great, good, and bad — that do require the last full measure of devotion. A reviewer's lot is not always an easy one. I can remember flogging myself to finish Harold Brodkey's *The Runaway Soul,* a novel of consummate, unmitigated tedium, interrupted by a few coloratura passages of great beauty and observation. Some people — not I — have complained about Proust's meandering sentences, Henry James's fine distinctions, or Thomas Aquinas's logic-chopping. Well, I say if you don't like them, don't read them. You're not in school any more. Even the best mountaineers aren't always up for an ascent of Mount Everest. Sometimes a reader just wants to spend some idle days on the Yann, or drift slowly along with Hercule Poirot as he solves some hideously complicated murder, or quietly revel in the mishaps of Bertie Wooster and Gussie Fink-Nottle. Just remember, though: keep trying books outside your comfort zone. At least from time to time. True readers boldly go where they haven't gone before.

3) Books don't just furnish a room. A personal library is a reflection of who you are and who you want to be, of what you value and what you desire, of how much you know and how much more you'd like to know. When I was growing up, there used to be an impressive librarian's guide entitled *Living with Books.* I think that's the right idea. Digital texts are all well and good, but books on shelves are a presence in your life. As such, they become a part of your day-to-day existence, reminding you, chastising you, calling to you. Plus, book collecting is, hands down, the greatest pastime in the world.

Well, I could go on with numbers four, five and six — whatever they might be. But I don't want to be overly pedantic or allow this farewell to go on too long. Elizabeth Bibesco once said that a goodbye, like a welcome, shouldn't be over-extended. "It is not the being together that it prolongs, it is the parting."

Still, I've never been able to write even a note to the milkman — back when there was a milkman — without a P.S. So just let me stress, one last time, that the world is full of wonderful stories, heartbreakingly beautiful and witty poems, thrilling works of history, biography, and philosophy. They will make you laugh, or hug yourself with pleasure, or deepen your thinking, or move you as profoundly as any experience this side of a serious love affair.

None of us, of course, will ever read all the books we'd like, but we can still make a stab at it. Why deny yourself all that pleasure? So look around tonight or this weekend, see what catches your fancy on the bookshelf, at the library, or in the bookstore. Maybe try something a little unusual, a little different. And then don't stop. Do it again, with a new book or an old author the following week. Go on — be bold, be insatiable, be restlessly, unashamedly promiscuous.

AFTERWORD

A freelance writer, by necessity, lurches from one deadline to the next. In looking back over this "year of reading, collecting and living with books" I should underscore that I often viewed these *Browsings* columns as a partial escape or temporary respite from my regular literary journalism. To round out this portrait of a bookman's year I thought it might be worth totting up the other writing I produced between February 2012 and February 2013. Many of the books or subjects listed below were chosen by me; perhaps a quarter were suggested by my editors.

Weekly Reviews for *The Washington Post* (These pieces — each about 1200 words long — appeared on Thursdays in the *Post*'s Style section)
Feb. 2 — *The Tender Hour of Twilight: Paris in the '50s, New York in the '60s, A Memoir*

2013

Jan. 3 — *Selected Letters of William Styron,* edited by Rose Styron with R. Blakeslee Gilpin

Jan. 10 — *The Balloonist,* by MacDonald Harris

Jan. 17 — *How to Live Like a Lord Without Really Trying,* by Shepherd Mead

Jan. 24 — *Trent: What Happened at the Council,* by John W. O'Malley

Jan. 31 — *Phantom Lady,* by Cornell Woolrich

Feb. 7 — *The Forgotten Writings of Bram Stoker,* edited by John Edgar Browning, and *The Lost Journal of Bram Stoker: The Dublin Years,* edited by Dacre Stoker and Elizabeth Miller

Feb. 14 — *The Real Jane Austen: A Life in Small Things,* by Paula Byrne

Feb. 21 — *Mute Poetry, Speaking Pictures,* by Leonard Barkan

Feb. 28 — *Robert Duncan: The Ambassador From Venus,* by Lisa Jarnot

The New York Review of Books
"Sherlock Lives!" — NYRB blog-essay on Sherlock Holmes and The Baker Street Irregulars, Feb. 2, 2012 [1,500 words]

"One of America's Best" — *The Devil's Dictionary, Tales, and Memoirs,* by Ambrose Bierce (Library of America), May 10, 2012 [Essay-review, 4,500 words]

"The Art of Revealing the Wreckage" — Richard Ford's *Canada,* July 12, 2012 [Essay-review, 3,500 words]

The *Times Literary Supplement*
Five essays about bookish matters for the TLS's "Freelance" column [each about 1,200 words, similar to the *Browsings* pieces]

Bookforum
[Reviews, approximately 1,500 words]
Distrust That Particular Favor, essays by William Gibson (December 2012)
The Atheist's Bible: The Most Dangerous Book That Never Existed, by Georges Minois (January 2013)

The Barnes and Noble Review
[These pieces appeared as part of my column "Library Without Walls" and generally ran about 2,500 words each]

"We Revel in Any Kind of Crowd: Dickens the Journalist," February 7, 2012
"A Dreamer of Mars: Edgar Rice Burroughs

and John Carter," March 9, 2012

Stranger Magic: Charmed States and the Arabian Nights, by Marina Warner, May 18, 2012

"Diamond in the Roughneck: The Books of Harry Crews," July 6, 2012

"Mediterranean Breeze": A Rediscovery of Norman Douglas's *South Wind,* August 10, 2012

Anti-Intellectualism in American Life, by Richard Hofstadter, Sept. 24, 2012

Religio Medici and Urne Burial, by Sir Thomas Browne, October 26, 2012

A Duckburg Holiday (three albums of Carl Barks's Uncle Scrooge and Donald Duck comics), December 24, 2012

The Purple Cloud, essay on the fiction of M. P. Shiel, February 1, 2013

The New Criterion

Philip Larkin: The Complete Poems, edited by Archie Burnett; April, 2012 [Essay-review, 2,500 words]

Library of America:

Online essay, of about 2,500 words, about *The Space Merchants,* by Frederik Pohl and Cyril Kornbluth, one of the novels reprinted in the LOA volume *American Science Fiction of the 1950s,* edited by

Gary Wolfe

Virginia Quarterly Review
Essay-review (of about 3,000 words) on *The Lifespan of a Fact,* by John D'Agata and Jim Fingal (Summer, 2012)

Harper's Magazine
"The Chameleon," an essay (3,000 words) on Thornton Wilder, Dec. 26, 2012.

The Weekly Standard
"Symons Says": 3,000-word essay on A. J. A. Symons, author of *The Quest for Corvo,* and Frederick Rolfe, author of *Hadrian VII* (December 17, 2012)

Lapham's Quarterly
Online essay (2,000 words) about three classics of "mystical" fiction: Arthur Machen's *The Hill of Dreams,* Walter de la Mare's *The Return,* and Algernon Blackwood's *The Centaur*

Reader's review of a manuscript for the University of Minnesota Press

"The Modern Adventure Novel" — A semester course, a follow-up to "The Classic Adventure Novel," taught as a visiting professor at the University of Maryland:

Edgar Rice Burroughs, *A Princess of Mars* (1912)

Rafael Sabatini, *Captain Blood* (1922)

Georgette Heyer, *These Old Shades* (1928)

Dashiell Hammett, *Red Harvest* (1929)

H. P. Lovecraft, *At the Mountains of Madness* (1931)

Eric Ambler, *A Coffin for Dimitrios* (1939)

Alfred Bester, *The Stars My Destination* (1956)

Chester Himes, *The Real Cool Killers* (1959)

Charles Portis, *True Grit* (1968)

William Goldman, *The Princess Bride* (1973)

Talks at Princeton University, the University of Maryland, the Howard County Poetry and Literature Society, and several schools and civic groups

BIOGRAPHICAL NOTE

Michael Dirda, a weekly book columnist for *The Washington Post,* is the author of *On Conan Doyle,* which received a 2012 Edgar Allan Poe Award from the Mystery Writers of America, and of the memoir *An Open Book,* which was honored with the 2004 Ohioana Award for nonfiction. Other works include four previous collections of essays: *Readings, Bound to Please, Book by Book* and *Classics for Pleasure.* Dirda graduated with highest honors in English from Oberlin College and earned a Ph.D. from Cornell University in comparative literature (with a concentration on medieval studies and European romanticism). He is a regular contributor to *The New York Review of Books,* the *Times Literary Supplement,* and the online *Barnes and Noble Review,* as well as a frequent reviewer for several other literary periodicals and an occasional lecturer and college teacher. In 1993 Dirda received the Pulitzer Prize for distinguished criticism. He and Marian Peck Dirda, senior prints and drawings conservator at the National Gallery of Art, live just outside of Washington, D.C. They have three grown sons.

ACKNOWLEDGMENTS

Robert Wilson, editor of *The American Scholar,* asked me to write these weekly essays. They were turned in to Sudip Bose who, when he wasn't saving me from error, provided wise counsel, encouragement and direction. I am grateful to them, and the staff of *The American Scholar* home page, for all their help and hard work on my behalf.

Browsings is dedicated to four of my "mentors," though I knew only Robert Phelps personally. As essayists and literary journalists, they showed me that one could discuss books with passion, intelligence and wit, and do so in a distinctly personal way. At various times in my life I read each of them avidly, seeking to understand how they created such genial, idiosyncratic presences on the page through style and diction alone. They're hardly to blame for my shortcomings, but they made me the writer I am.

Finally, I am grateful for the enthusiasm and contributions of everyone at Pegasus, starting with Claiborne Hancock, Jessica Case, Iris Blasi and Maria Fernandez. You have all been wonderful. The handsome dust jacket design of *Browsings* should be credited to Michael Fusco Straub. Not least, Ed Perlman long ago encouraged me to give my original columns a more permanent form. My agents Glen Hartley and Lynn Chu then guided and advised me with their usual spirit and acumen. Thank you all for helping turn these bite-sized literary entertainments into a book.

ABOUT THE AUTHOR

Michael Dirda is a Pulitzer Prize–winning critic and longtime book columnist for *The Washington Post.* He was once chosen by *Washingtonian Magazine* as one of the twenty-five smartest people in our nation's capital (but, as Michael says, you have to consider the competition). He also writes regularly for the *Times Literary Supplement;* the *New York Review of Books* and other literary journals. His previous publications include the memoir *An Open Book,* four collections of essays — *Readings, Bound to Please, Book by Book,* and *Classics for Pleasure* — and *On Conan Doyle,* for which he won a 2012 Edgar Award. A lifelong Sherlock Holmes and Conan Doyle fan, he was inducted into The Baker Street Irregulars in 2002. He lives in Silver Spring, Maryland.